A MAN FACING THE MATTERHORN

is no ordinary man, especially if he has within him a desire for conquest. Some of the great pioneers, Whymper in particular, have written the story of their adventures. Rather than paraphrase these accounts, as has been done many times, I have chosen to quote long extracts from them as often as possible; thus the temperament, the thought, and sometimes the philosophy of each of them appear unaltered.

Certain of these passages come from books, magazines or newspapers, several of which are little known and hard to find because they have long been out of print. It has been my pleasure to collect them together. Paul Payot and André Wahl readily agreed to help me; I thank them cordially. I am grateful also to Bradford Washburn, whose remarkable aerial photographs illustrate several pages of this work.

While writing this book I have lived night and day with the Matterhorn, the legendary mountain; I have been roped with the pioneers, all great characters. This is no mean privilege, and I appreciate my good fortune.

More completely detached from its setting than any other mountain, pure and solitary, the Matterhorn is the most beautiful peak in the world. And what beautifies it still more is the love that fragile men have brought to it; what lends beauty to a pyramid of rock surrounded by glaciers is the smile that is in our hearts.

3

4

GASTON RÉBUFFAT

MEN AND

Cover
The Matterhorn. Photo: Heimhuber

Pages 2-3
The south face of the Matterhorn, seen from the property
of Guido Rey at Breuil. Photo: Hubert Cretton

Pages 4-5
The east face of the Matterhorn, seen from the path from
the Bétemps hut. Photo: Pierre Bichet

Pages 6-7
The Matterhorn, upper section of the west face.
Photo: Bradford Washburn

Page 9
On the north face of the Matterhorn. Photo: Georges Tairraz

First published in the USA 1967
by Oxford University Press Inc,
200 Madison Avenue,
New York, N.Y. 10016.

Revised edition 1973

ISBN 0 19 519059 9
Library of Congress Catalog Card Number 67-11409

All enquiries and requests relevant to this title should be sent to
the publisher at the above address, not to the printer.

Printed in Italy.

THE MATTERHORN

TRANSLATED FROM THE FRENCH
BY ELEANOR BROCKETT

NEW YORK
OXFORD UNIVERSITY PRESS
1973

THE CLASSIC PEAK

'The most beautiful sight this region offers is the proud and lofty peak of the Matterhorn, which rises to an enormous height in the form of a triangular obelisk of living rock, and which seems to have been carved with a chisel.' So declared Horace Bénédict de Saussure when, in 1789, in the course of his travels in the Alps, he went from Breuil to Zermatt, crossing the Théodule Pass, where he bivouacked. All the peaks of the Valais were around him, but he made his choice.

Profoundly moved, he added: 'I promise myself that I will come back another year to examine and measure this magnificent crag at closer range. But it will not be measured by taking a barometer up it; for its sheer sides offer no possibility of access and do not even afford a hold for the snow.'

Beauty and inaccessibility were the two impressions that de Saussure registered at the sight of the amazing and impregnable Matterhorn. Since that time, or more precisely, since the first ascent in 1865, millions of people have admired it and thousands have climbed it; the four ridges and the four faces have been climbed, direct routes have been traced out, and even a traverse around the 'head' of the Matterhorn has been accomplished. Nevertheless, nothing has changed; each time you arrive at Zermatt or Breuil and raise your head at last to see the

peak you have been dreaming about night and day, such is the magnetism of the mountain that you are struck to the very depth of your being.

You follow a track, and you draw nearer; one step, then another, and your spirit, no less than your body, is in motion. You have just left the village, with its hustle and its security, to cross a border, invisible but strongly felt, to penetrate a silence, to enter upon an intimacy. You stop, you listen, you sense a certain quality in things: the taste of the air, the sun enveloping the mountain, the undulation of the meadows, the camber of the moraine, the curves of the glaciers. The other peaks are beautiful—the Matterhorn is a presence. You survey the way it divides the winds and rends the clouds; you question it. It reigns and governs. Its simple shape, its uncompromising ridges, are the pre-conditions of its solitude: to live alone, if you wish to preserve your integrity, you have to be doubly strong. The Matterhorn is protected by no other mountains. It is a law unto itself. It does not share the air it breathes.

For a moment a gust of wind flattens the grass around you; up above there, the north wind is rising. And you indulge in reverie about the great millenary earth tremors, the shocks and foldings, the convulsions, thrusts and collapses which threw up this mountain, symbol of the will, born of happy chance—or was it of a precise command?—today offered to mankind, welcomed but springing unexpectedly from its terrestrial trap-door like a jack-in-the-box.

The miracle is permanent: emotion immediately takes

left-hand page
The east face of the Matterhorn. Photo: Swissair

pages 14-15
The east face of the Matterhorn. Photo: Heimhuber

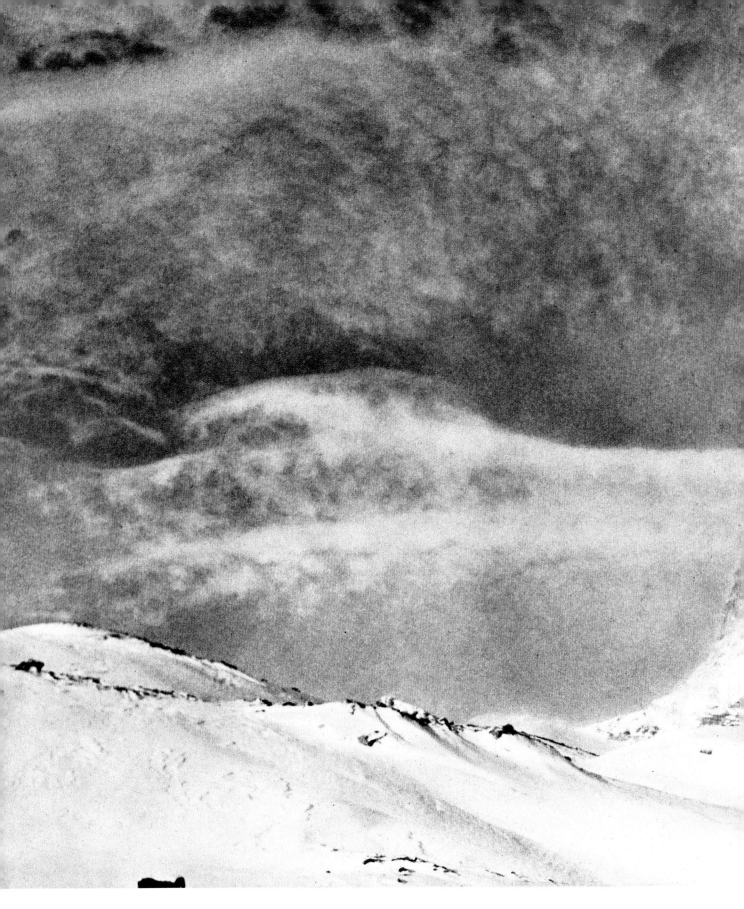

over from aesthetic satisfaction: the fusion of beauty and inaccessibility is indissoluble. Closely backed by another mountain, or jostling the Monte Rosa, the Weisshorn or the Mishabels, the Matterhorn, despite its classic lines, would no longer be this extraordinary beacon-light, this thrust of rock, this aspiration of earth towards heaven.

Alone, but with lines at the same time less regular and less pure, with – let us suppose for a moment – ridges which were very beautiful but out of true, asymmetric, contorted, divided, weighted with turrets and cluttered with gendarmes, the Matterhorn, despite its isolation, would become a mountain like the others, whereas, by virtue of its situation and its austerity it is unique. 'What power must have been required to shatter and to sweep away the missing parts of this pyramid; for we do not see it surrounded by heaps of fragments; one sees only other peaks – themselves rooted to the ground – whose sides, equally rent, indicate an immense mass of débris, of which we do not see any trace in the neighbourhood. Doubtless this is that débris which, in the form of pebbles, boulders and sand, fills our valleys and the beds of our lakes where they come down, some by way of the Valais, others by way of the valley of Aosta, on the Lombardy side,' wrote de Saussure on the occasion of his second journey in 1792 to the Théodule Pass. Face to face with the Matterhorn, with this work of art accomplished over thousands of years, how can one refrain from dreaming?

*

The sculptor had at his disposal on that occasion an immense and magnificent block of stone; but from that block, scorning any parcelling out of his material, he made only one summit.

Up to that time he had carved – or planned to carve – rocky peaks, hills, needles, crags, steeples and turrets, many of which were of great beauty, especially extraordinary walls like the west face of the Drus, the north face of the Grandes Jorasses, the Eiger or the Cime Grande di Lavaredo, or ridges as pure and strong as the Spigolo Giallo della Piccola or the south ridge of the Aiguille Noire de Peuterey. Indeed, these mountains were very beautiful, but they were remarkable first and foremost because of certain parts of their architecture or their ornamentation which contrived to surpass the work as a whole: certain sides were sublime, while others had been forgotten or negligently executed, either because the sculptor had lacked space or because he had allowed himself to be swayed by other considerations. He had concentrated his genius on areas of the mountain to the detriment, as it were, of the mountain itself. When you look at the Drus, you 'see' the west face; when you look at the Aiguille Noire de Peuterey, you 'see' the south ridge. This time, he wanted to create, not a conglomeration of walls and ridges, some of great beauty and others of inferior merit, fixed to a single mountain, but a balanced, harmonious peak with walls and ridges equal without being identical, contributing to the mountain and not to their own greater glory; later, in the world of men, this would come to be called the 'team spirit'. When men looked at the Matterhorn from whatever direction, north, south, east or west, they would see nothing else! Afterwards, long afterwards, on applying their minds to it they would notice that it had ridges and faces like other peaks.

The sculptor was ready to try his hand: the mountain would not be a giant, but it would have grandeur; its height would be moderate, its shape would be pure and balanced, strong and harmonious. He knew that he could not succeed by virtuosity or power, but by simplicity, almost by starkness. He wished, not merely to create a mountain, but to lay bare its very soul.

What a wild dream!

How many times had he tried before, without ever succeeding! At least, in the course of his countless experiments, he had learned that the path of balance and simplicity of form, as in the drop of water or the point of a crystal, is the hardest to find – and to follow.

He oriented his subject; it must be seen from Zermatt or from Breuil, and from the peaks of the Valais without being higher than they were.

Then, with a decisiveness and a vigour of which he had been incapable until that moment, he created emptiness all round to a great distance, sacrificing the possibility of ten other peaks; the mountain would be alone, isolated! For a long time he prepared the ground. He had the strength not to waver. Then he swept away the stone chippings, and having cleared the ground, he knew peace. But almost immediately he felt the weight of responsibility: after such prodigality, the work which was to result from the remaining block must be perfect.

Frightened for a moment, then happy, (for he was strong), he set to work determined to create the dream mountain. And yet straightway, he who had succeeded in creating marvels felt clumsy and, at first, disoriented. His design was so simple that he could not manage to bring it into being. Face to face with the stone, he found himself powerless, not knowing how to attack it. It is true that he did not lack experience, he had built and chiselled thousands of majestic walls, finely crenelated ridges, but he knew well in his innermost being that this time his way did not lie in that direction.

When evening came, he lay down facing the stars, fell asleep and dreamed once again. He clung to his dream with all his might.

In the morning when the sun rose far to the east, the north wind was blowing very strongly, virile and cold. He wanted to collect his thoughts, but the more he tried to do so and set them in order the more they escaped him. He looked at the sky. On certain stormy days, the clouds had assumed for a moment the shape of that ideal mountain; but clouds like dreams, lose their shape so quickly! The wind was icy; to warm himself he set to work: the steel of the chisel stuck to his fingers. Then he suddenly felt that his fingers were coming to life, and that an instinct was guiding them; an energetic force was flowing within him, henceforward something incorruptible inspired him. The image of this mountain, carried confusedly within him for so long, was about to come to birth little by little under his chisel. He felt it and experienced from it a great joy, a warmth, and the thought that this was happiness. Then, so as not to waver, he made absolute accuracy his principle; he gave himself to his work, body and soul; his will was concentrated upon it, his passion became all-consuming.

His chisel was more active than he was himself. Under blows delivered spontaneously, he adjusted the height of the summit, he cleared the crest, gave the walls their slope, and the ridges formed at their intersection. As he carved, he moved around the block; it was the first time he had been able to work in this way. That, too, was a new and wonderful discovery for him; now, having committed himself, he was still surprised and frightened by his own audacity in having razed and swept away everything around; but straightway he recalled the two salient points of his dream; that lonely, isolated mountain, very beautiful because very simple.

In fact he noticed that he was in the process of carving four walls facing the four cardinal points, and he was afraid for a moment that too much regularity would lead to an unacceptable monotony. In short, in work of this kind he was a novice, like a child. A child, however, is afraid of nothing, while he had so much experience. He reflected or, rather, he day-dreamed; his work should aim at unity not uniformity. On the other hand, if he gave play to his imagination he would risk losing control of the walls; they would tend to be sucked in or to belly out, he must watch dangerously individualistic ridges which would obtrude, to the detriment of the whole design.

He knew what he did *not* want to do but how could he create the work of which he dreamed?

Elsewhere, more than once he had had moments of weakness, temptations, impulses. In distress, he moved once more around the block of stone. The violent wind blew with great force. He took his chisel again and, finding peace once more, he resumed his carving. Again his fingers rather than he himself were in control. Little by little, feeling intuitively what he wanted, he slipped back into his dream: to create a mountain, not ridges and faces, multiple, varied and with a taste for independence. No wall, no ridge should be privileged or neglected; all should be equal but not interchangeable, each having its *raison d'être*, its own character, its own orientation, its way of playing with the sun, the wind and the storms, or welcoming the stars, none of them being very outstanding in any way except in its pure, ascetic profile, accepting the self-effacement of striving only for the elegance and harmony of the whole mountain. To create a mountain, not a series of incidental ornaments, that was his clear purpose.

So he mastered the ridges, prone to vanity, always ready to parade themselves, craving to be prominent and well to the fore, to thrust themselves forward, to seize their opportunity selfishly, quick to flee, to find themselves again, to run, to bend, to twist, to proliferate, to disappear, to rebound, like a stone serpent that slips between the fingers.

He controlled the walls, prone to pride, which, to increase their width, try to push back, to separate the ridges. He stripped them of all decoration, baring the

pages 18-19
The south face of the Matterhorn.
Photo: Bradford Washburn

strength of their line, the quivering of their spines as sun and winds passed over them.

He returned to the ridges, adventurous by vocation, mindful lest any of the four, breaking its moorings, should stretch, lengthen, stray or spread, escaping so as to win a selfish advantage; and, by pulling the edifice towards itself, should endanger its balance and topple it over.

He eliminated pillars, columns, spurs; he denied himself towers and even lacework of rock, so beautiful in itself, but also inclined to attract the eye and monopolise attention for itself alone, effeminate, over-refined, admirable elsewhere, but out of place here.

A second time he knew peace; his dream was there, facing him, from whatever angle he looked at it. Setting aside all adventurousness, rejecting a thousand possibilities, he experienced the joy of renunciation; his art had been to subdue and master his own impulses as well as those of the stone, until this or that ridge would no longer be noticed, until there were no longer ridges attached to a summit and walls hung between them, but a balanced and harmonious whole, of extraordinary vigour, as if it had emerged effortlessly from the earth just as it was.

*

I was born by the sea, and up to the age of twelve I had never been outside my native Provence; and yet, without being aware of it, I knew the Matterhorn. I did not know it by name, but I knew it. When, by chance, someone in my family uttered the word 'peak', and my small child's imagination created the corresponding picture, I saw a pyramid, beautiful as an arrow of stone, pointing towards the sky.

At school, at the very outset, when the master was teaching us how to hold a pencil and, to amuse us, would say, 'Now, draw a house, a tree, a flower, a boat, a mountain,' all of us without knowing or intending it, would draw Matterhorns.

Later, in the Alps, in the Himalayas, in the Rockies, on the Hoggar, I have been up countless valleys to discover mountains of all shapes and heights, but have never come across any like the Matterhorn. I have questioned climbers of all countries who have visited even more of the world's mountains than I have. They have never seen a mountain to compare with the Matterhorn either. Moreover, on reflection, no one arriving at Zermatt or coming up from Châtillon to Breuil has ever exclaimed on seeing the Matterhorn for the first time,

'It looks like such and such a mountain,' even a mountain wearing the halo of the Himalayas. Besides, this statement does not ring true, it is so clearly impossible.

Conversely, on approaching other peaks, how many times have we said, spontaneously and with a peculiar joy, 'Seen from here it looks like the Matterhorn,' or 'Seen from there, that curve of the ridge, that profile of the wall reminds one of the Matterhorn.'

No, the Matterhorn can resemble no other peak – it is the model; similarly, no other peak really resembles the Matterhorn; the mould has been broken, there are not even any copies. The Matterhorn is unique!

*

'From childhood I have had the most decided passion for mountains.' How many of us have not experienced this sharp and imperative feeling expressed by de Saussure – and, it must be said, with the solemn happiness which gives orientation to life?

More than a hundred years before the first ascent of the Matterhorn, the young naturalist had a revelation. Up to that time mountains, sterile and useless, cluttered the sky and blocked the horizon. Now, in 1760, facing and contemplating Mont Blanc from the Brévent, which he had just climbed, de Saussure was seized by a great desire, a slightly mad desire: to get to the summit of the great dome of snow, halfway to the sky. At that time it was 'not done' to climb mountains, it was unthinkable, especially for a person of his rank! Science came to the young man's rescue: it would be a justification for a barely-mentionable undertaking; he would go to Mont Blanc to read his barometer. The excuse mattered little; that day a great adventure began: de Saussure gave a new dimension to the earth, that of vertical lines, and created a new passion, the passion that draws men towards the peaks.

Twenty-six years later, Doctor Paccard and a collector of crystals named Jacques Balmat reached the summit of Mont Blanc. The following year, on 1 August 1787, the scientist himself, with exemplary love and tenacity, gained for himself at the age of forty-seven the

right-hand page
On the Hörnli ridge, with the Dent Blanche in the background. Photo: Pierre Tairraz
pages 22-23
The Matterhorn.
Litho: Gabriel Loppé, from the collection of Paul Payot

well-merited joy and satisfaction of climbing the great dome of snow in his turn. He returned happy, but he did not stop at that; promptly the following year, indefatigable, still fanatically keen, he continued his climbs, his studies and his observations.

In 1789 he undertook his sixth journey in the Alps with the aim of 'exploring the region of Monte Rosa, which has been for a long time the object of my curiosity', as he wrote. The region and the Monte Rosa interested him – the Matterhorn surprised, enchanted and inspired him. In 1792 he came back again – the seventh and last journey – to 'see again and to study in detail the topmost summit of the Matterhorn'. His love of mountains, revealed on Mont Blanc, was to end with the Matterhorn, which filled him with awe, and which he judged to be unclimbable. Seven years later, at the age of only fifty-nine, he was to die, worn out by his journeys, but with his heart's desire fulfilled.

Nowadays, to go from Breuil to Zermatt by crossing the Théodule Pass, as de Saussure did in 1789, is no longer a feat: the mountain is equipped with mechanical ski-lifts, and from December to May countless skiers make enjoyable descents of suitable slopes. In summer, too, you can use the cableways which form a continuation of the road that climbs up to Breuil, or of the railway line that goes as far as Zermatt. Let us, however, take our time and make the journey on foot with de Saussure:

'At three-quarters of a league from the waterfall, one arrives at Valtournanche, a large parish composed of several separate hamlets surrounded by cultivated plots on steep slopes, supported here and there by walls, with rye and oats which were then being harvested; so that the countryside appeared extremely animated. Above these cultivated slopes the mountains on either side of the village are very steep; and ahead, to the north, the parish seems closed in by mountains that form a semi-circular wall . . .

'From there, within an hour, you come to the chalets of Breuil, 1,027 fathoms high, by way of marshy meadows

of little gradient, following the stream of the Matterhorn.

'Breuil is a summer hamlet. We met again there our good host Erin; but also our small and evil bedroom without bed or window, a kitchen without a chimney, and all the privations and little discomforts which, added together, do not fail to cause a great deal of annoyance.

'The next day, in the early morning, we sent Marie Couttet, with three men of Breuil, to prepare for us at the top of the col a dwelling which, despite their good offices, was to prove even less comfortable than that of Breuil; and to give them the time to prepare it, we did not leave until about nine o'clock.'

Towards the middle of the afternoon, having scaled the grassy slopes, then the moraines and the glacier, de Saussure arrived at the Théodule Pass. 'One enjoys a very beautiful view here,' writes the naturalist. 'The situation is magnificent, and the surrounding mountains vie with one another in beauty, but the most awe-inspiring, the most extraordinary, is the proud and lofty peak of the Matterhorn, which rises to an enormous height in the form of a triangular obelisk of living rock, and which seems to have been carved with a chisel.'

'The col itself,' writes de Saussure, 'is a curiosity: it is a fort or redoubt in the form of a defensive wall of dry stones very firmly placed, with loopholes for large muskets. This redoubt bears the name of St Théodule; we have already seen another above the entrance to the glacier. These two redoubts were built two or three centuries ago by the inhabitants of the Val d'Aosta, who feared an invasion from that direction by the inhabitants of the Valais. They are probably the most highly-situated fortifications on our planet. Alas, that men should have erected in these high regions such a durable work, only as a monument to their hatred and their destructive passions.'

The camp was pitched slightly to the east of the col: 'The evening was very cold, and we had great difficulty in lighting a fire,' de Saussure goes on. 'Our guides had brought neither tinder nor matches; I believe, indeed, that in Breuil these inventions are considered luxuries, and we would certainly not have managed to light one had we not had gunpowder and ether. Despite this fire, we suffered greatly from the cold. However, we warmed up under our fur-lined cloaks, and we passed a very good night.'

The following day was devoted to trigonometrical measurement of the 'Needle of the Matterhorn'. De

Saussure arrived at a figure of 2,309·75 fathoms, which is 14,609 feet, a remarkable result when one thinks that the height of the Matterhorn is 14,800 feet.

Then de Saussure studied the structure of the extraordinary pyramid: 'However favourable I am towards the theory of crystallization, it seems to me impossible to believe that such an obelisk could have emerged in this form from the hands of nature with cleanly-cut strata on its sides; for we certainly have here, not a crystal or a single stone, but an agglomerate of superimposed strata of very different natures.'

A day of study, and also of meditation for the scientist: 'But who, by plausible conjecture, can penetrate the smallest distance into the darkness of the ages? Placed on this planet yesterday, and for one day only, we can only long for knowledge that we shall probably never attain.'

The next day de Saussure climbed the little peak that dominates the col to continue his observations: the temperature, the colour of the sky, the insect life . . . Then came the descent to Zermatt.

'The sight of this village, surrounded by woods and beautiful meadows, gives a keen pleasure at the moment when one espies it from the middle of the glacier; it gently rests eyes and mind wearied by seeing nothing but snow and arid rocks.

'We had extreme difficulty in finding a house where they were willing to put us up; the innkeepers were either absent or ill-disposed. The priest who sometimes gives travellers lodging sent the reply that he was unwilling to do business with us. In the end our worthy guide Jean-Baptiste Erin compelled an innkeeper to take us.'

Times have certainly changed, and now Zermatt is one of the most hospitable resorts.

'The peak of the Matterhorn, although about two or three leagues distant from this village, seems to tower majestically above it, and so the village gives it its name in the Valais countryside, where it is called Matterhorn, or Horn of Matt.'

Years passed. Timidly at first, then systematically, in particular with the impetus given by the Alpine Club founded in London in 1857, the attack was launched on all the peaks. One after the other, all were climbed. But the Matterhorn was still there, unconquered, the cynosure of attention. The Matterhorn challenge was to become the Matterhorn obsession. With its classic shape it haunted the days and nights of all. Many cherished the desire to try; some actually made the attempt. There remained only the most determined: those who somehow resembled the Matterhorn, who were of the same 'blood'; Whymper's jaw, Carrel's gaze were of the Matterhorn stamp.

It was a contest, but also a love story and perhaps something of a detective story. The Englishman and the guide from Valtournanche were to make plans, carry out reconnaissances, make trial climbs; the two men were sometimes to set out together, but finally each would make the attempt on his own account.

The fourteenth of July 1865 was to be the dénouement. Whymper was to reach the summit by way of the Swiss ridge; but drama was to follow hard upon victory.

From the other side, three days later, Carrel and Bich were to arrive at the top by way of the Italian ridge: a 'grande première' which was, however, only a second.

Perhaps, even certainly, the ascent would have been achieved without accident if the Englishman and the Italian had roped up together. There might have been a happy ending. But Fate, unpredictable as the mountain, was to play its part. Whymper and Carrel wanted victory too much to contemplate losing it or sharing it.

left-hand page
Horace-Bénédict de Saussure
Lithograph by luel, from the collection of Paul Payot

Pages 30-31
The Matterhorn from Riffelalp. Photo: Heimhuber

pages 32-33
The Matterhorn from the Théodule Pass
Drawing by Edward Whymper; photo: Hachette

THE ATTEMPTS

In 1860, when he discovered the Matterhorn, Edward Whymper was twenty, the same age as Horace-Bénédict de Saussure a century earlier when from the Brévent he had dreamed of the ascent of Mont Blanc. How different they were!

Whymper did not dream of the ascent: he desired it— and he was impatient. A London publisher had commissioned him to make sketches of the great Alpine peaks; he went to Switzerland, Italy and France. The peaks were beautiful, and moreover, some had still to be conquered. He climbed Mont Pelvoux, as he was to climb other peaks: the Dolent, the Aiguille de Trélatête, the Aiguille d'Argentière, and even the Aiguille Verte; these were just stages in his quest, and if, almost by mistake, he dreamed for a moment, it was of climbing 'the most inaccessible of all the mountains': the Matterhorn.

The elegant and haughty pyramid figured on his programme, and already . . . on his list of honours. 'However magnificent dreams of the imagination may be, they always remain inferior to reality,' Whymper wrote. The young Englishman was not going to fog his mind with marvellous daydreams; he was not going to indulge in agreeable mental wanderings. From that moment the man with the steely gaze was in action: he had no time to lose. The Alpine Club had been in existence for three years. The impetus had been given in formal style. Rivalry reached the highest pitch of intensity. English-

men had already carried out reconnaissances—T. S. Kennedy in 1858, Vaughan Hawkins with the Swiss guide Johann Joseph Bennen in 1859. Englishmen had even attempted the ascent—the three Parker brothers, without a guide, reached a height of nearly 12,000 feet on the Hörnli ridge in 1860. But before them some Italians, men from the Val d'Aosta, had been the first to make the venture; to do so they had had to overcome certain fears. 'There are stories as ancient and beautiful as mythology,' Guido Rey points out in his book on the Matterhorn. 'No one knows how they came into being. They are an odd mixture of pagan and Christian ideas, vestiges of tradition that persist in mountain regions more tenaciously than elsewhere. There are the ordinary stories of fairies, or pixies, dancing in circles at dawn on grass pearly with dew, on which they leave traces of their joyous rout; stories of wandering souls from purgatory appearing at night as will o' the wisps in the calm meanderings of the mountain stream; there are also tales of miserly dwarfs who, at the twilight hour, come out of the cave where their hoard is hidden; from far off, precious stones and gold can be seen scattered among the rocks, shining and twinkling in the last rays of the sun. The thought of riches hidden away in the fastnesses of the mountain has always excited the imagination and the cupidity of the poor mountain-dwellers. And near certain mysterious rocks, in almost inaccessible places, are still

Edward Whymper. From the collection of Emile Gos

34

to be found the traces of their arduous, deluded searches.

'They all knew that up there, by the Becca – as they called the Matterhorn – where the storms took shape and where rose the clouds, black as the smoke of hell, which brought the storm, was the devil in person: he it was who continually hurled masses of rock down into the valley.'

Reared in this atmosphere, having neither the money nor the time to waste on mountain climbing, it is quite remarkable and exceptional in the history of the peaks that the local folk, alone, without the aid of a rich tourist, should have taken the initiative to set out for the Matterhorn. The only encouragement they received came from Canon Carrel, who lived in Aosta, an erudite and respected man interested in the natural sciences, who received foreign visitors, and who was doubtless the first to realize what a great tourist attraction and source of income the famous mountain could become for the high valley of Breuil, at that time so poverty-stricken.

So it was that three of them, all relations of the canon, left Valtournanche separately and secretly so as not to arouse suspicion – Jean-Jacques Carrel, a great chamois-hunter, Amé Gorret, a seminarist, and Jean-Antoine Carrel, the 'Bersagliere', who happened to be in the village between the two battles of Novare and Solferino. They met at the chalet of Avouil, climbed the first slopes, and arrived at the summit of the Tête du Lion (about 12,000 feet), the first spur of the Italian ridge of the Matterhorn. They contemplated the Matterhorn, looked at their village, then on the other slope their eyes fell, not on the valley of Hérens, as they had expected, but on an immense glacier surrounded by high peaks; they rolled stones down to get some idea of the drop. By climbing the Tête du Lion instead of going round it, they had taken the wrong route; but it mattered little; they were as happy as children; impelled by a great passion, they were the first men to have set out for the Matterhorn!

The same summer two other men from the Val d'Aosta, Gabriel Maquignaz and Victor Carrel, followed their example and also made an attempt.

The following year Jean-Antoine and Jean-Jacques Carrel set out for a fresh assault, and it is thought that they reached the base of the Grande Tour at 12,992 feet, the spot where the Luigi Amedeo hut stands today – a magnificent achievement considering the poorness of their equipment.

So, thanks to the intelligence of the Canon and the courage of a few of the modest inhabitants of Valtournanche, the first step had been taken. The formerly unthinkable idea of climbing the Matterhorn was born in the minds of the Valtorneans.

Carrel, born in 1829, was eleven years older than Whymper. He, too, had eyes of steel, but in addition, and to the detriment of his efficiency, he had, despite his appearance, a soft spot. Between him and the famous mountain there was more than a desire for conquest; there was a bond of affection, a kinship; the Matterhorn had seen him being born and growing up.

Every day of his childhood and his youth Jean-Antoine had gazed at and admired the Matterhorn, even on those days when it was hidden by clouds. His young life had been dominated by it, and when, after eight long years of military service, the 'Bersagliere' returned to Valtournanche and found his mountain again, his determination to climb it by the face that overlooked his valley became stronger every day.

However, Carrel was not wealthy – far from it! That was why, although he was a hunter rather than a guide, he came to offer his services for hire. As much through natural pride as independence of spirit, he wished, when he succeeded, to be not merely the wonderful instrument that the guide was at that period, but also the decision-maker and commander. It was not enough for him to be the best climber of the moment, the first man on the rope; he wanted to be the boss. If Carrel guided Whymper to the summit, he would run the risk, despite his qualities, of playing only a secondary role, for Whymper had an overbearing personality. Indeed, even today, when there is mention of the Matterhorn, one immediately thinks of Whymper. Yet Michael Croz played an important part in the first ascent: he it was who led the victorious team; moreover, Whymper, in his accounts, never failed to say so and to acknowledge the exceptional qualities of the guide from Chamonix; nevertheless, Croz is hardly known.

Carrel was to agree sometimes to being roped with Whymper; the attempts he made with the Englishman brought him a little money, and enabled him to take the measure of his rival while improving his own knowledge of the terrain; but Carrel never gave the impression that he wished to push an attempt in Whymper's company to a conclusion.

The Englishman's intentions, on the other hand, were

not ringed about with any special considerations. He had not been born at the foot of the Matterhorn, on either one side or the other; it mattered little to him whether the 'inaccessible peak' was called Cervin or Matterhorn or whether it was there or elsewhere. To climb it, any of the faces would do, and to get there he was ready to be roped with Carrel any time he wished, and indeed, with anyone at all, or almost, as on the day of the first ascent. All this is readily understandable, especially in a cold, efficient character like Whymper's.

In 1860, let us remember, the young Englishman was twenty years old; from the age of fifteen he had kept a diary, from which Frank Smythe has published extracts: 'One sees in them the life of a child of precocious intelligence, who reads *The Times* daily and considers the news with the unshakable good sense, scepticism and dryness of a thirty-year-old subscriber:

'*2 February 1855.* Today the Ministers resigned in consequence of a motion by Mr Roebuck in the House of Commons to inquire into the conduct of the war, and the ministers, not wanting an inquiry, resigned. However, there will be one. The Queen sent for Lord Derby, but he refused to try and form a cabinet because Mr Gladstone and Lord Palmerston would not take office under him. The popular voice is for Lord Palmerston, but he has very little favour in the Queen's eyes. A cold day and snowing.

'*2 November 1855.* No news. The mortality and illness generally of London has, for the last few months, been much under the average, insomuch that the doctors are complaining that they have nothing to do . . .

'*17 February 1856, Sunday.* Heard a Mr Rosevere of Coventry preach. A very good preacher, and would have been asked to preach again, had not his congregation sent up by electric telegraph for him to come back. Another murder (at Portsmouth).'

'Day after day,' observes Claire-Eliane Engel in her excellent preface to the French edition of Whymper's *Scrambles amongst the Alps*, 'the entries run on in unbroken succession: the Crimean War, then the peace negotiations, railway accidents, suicides, the Indian Mutiny, the launching of the *Leviathan,* financial crises and bankruptcies, always from the *Times.* Edward Whymper went to church twice each Sunday, played cricket and followed the important matches of this national sport; the whole week he carved blocks for his father, who was a wood engraver. He travelled little – Brighton, Hastings, later the Lake District. He went to hear the nigger minstrels, and was present at magic lantern sessions at which Albert Smith showed "The Ascent of Mont Blanc" in his shadow-theatre. One can sense how much this monotonous life played on his nerves. He got on very well indeed with his parents, even with his step-mother when his father remarried after his mother's death. He was very close to his brothers and sisters. However, that does not constitute an aim in life. He became turned in upon himself, champed at the bit, and by so doing gradually managed to destroy in himself all sensibility, all emotion that might rise to the surface, all sentimental impulses. He had no friends, and was never to have any. At fifteen, at twenty, at sixty, he was to remain self-contained; his mind was rigid, hard, meticulous, sufficient unto itself, and secret. He never confided in anyone.'

On 14 July 1865, Whymper reached the summit of the

above
Zermatt and its old chalets. Drawing by E. Rubino
pages 38-39
Sunset. Photo: Bradford Washburn

BICHET.

South face of the Matterhorn; on the left, Lion arête;
on the right, Furggen arête.
Drawing by Pierre Bichet

'inaccessible peak': a great victory, but soon afterwards, during the descent, a terrible catastrophe; Whymper was obliged to write to *The Times* to 'present the facts and to refute all manner of melodramatic accusations. He was then twenty-four and these letters show a degree of self-control, a maturity of spirit and a dignity rare even among men a good deal older'.

Six years later, in 1871, his book *Scrambles amongst the Alps* appeared. It was a great and immediate success. Now, before taking part in the great adventure with this extraordinary man, and in order thoroughly to understand with whom we are going to be roped, let us hear the great English alpinist Geoffrey Winthrop Young speak of the book and the author: 'The Whymper, whose early life, as I now read it in the Diaries, and whose long post-Matterhorn life of self-exploitation can be assigned quite simply to a particular nineteenth century period and class and type, refuses to become identified with the heroic figure whose *Scrambles Amongst the Alps* suddenly blared like a destroying Trumpet round my narrow school walls, scattering them to all the four corners of a blue firmament behind high icy peaks. How did a personality so seemingly limited succeed in capturing the imagination of so many hundreds of us, in succeeding generations, with his one book? Was there possibly something even in the nature of his limitations as a man which, when he came to write, left his message free of the convention of the period, or even gave it an unconventional appeal? Whymper, as we re-read him, we see to have been inferior to most of his fellow prophets in sensibility, in imagination, and in culture. His love of giving information might be expected to be boring to youth, and the artistry of his book, for all his work upon it, is patchy. And yet there are very few works upon a single and out of the way theme which have continued to be read with such enduring zest. His secret, does it lie in his fidelity? in his power of visualizing himself and his surroundings in words of snapshot precision, so that we feel it is all just happening to ourselves? We take part, dramatically, in the conflict in progress, on our one hand the obstinacy of the man, on our other the reality of the forces against him. It is the same relationship with hills, at once sympathetic and antagonistic, which we all come to know as mountaineers; and it is kept vividly before us, the flashlight representation of a flinty mountain and of a steely Whymper in continuous concussion; all illuminated by the sparks of perilous incident they struck out of one another. Whymper is egocentric: he never sees himself detachedly or as anywhere but in the centre of a picture; he seems to feel little but surface emotion and no sentiment; he reveals himself as a man unresponsive in relationships, either human or with nature; he is bold, self-confident and calculating. His mind, that of a first-rate journalist rather ahead of his period, governed an unimaginative and not wholly amiable temperament . . . Whymper in life, and Whymper as a writer, was an honest egoist; he wrote himself–"the book is entirely personal, all ego!" But nowhere in mountain literature do we receive a like impression of the unendingness of the mountain quest, or of the insignificance of the individual in comparison with it . . . .

' . . . . All the time he is shouting at us "These are the Mountains and this is Me!–and thus went the truth that passed between us!" And while he postures and proclaims, he succeeds in representing the mountains as so very big, and the charm and the business of the mountaineering hunt as so infinitely enduring, that we almost lose sight of himself in the course of his own domineering narrative. Only in the end to find that we have practically confused him with the Matterhorn . . . . .

'After the accident there was to be no escape from his role as the premier mountaineer. The resounding tragedy coming as the close of a type of novel adventure in itself alarming to the safe Victorian age, gave him an international fame and fortune. Its sombre halo never again forsook him. As a journalist, an illustrator, and ambitious, it was inevitable that he should follow where fate pointed so obvious a way. There was something also in his rugged but static personality, which kept him for the remainder of his life unalterably in the public eye, as still the only surviving conqueror of the Matterhorn, still impersonating as he came and went, the historic catastrophe.'

1861

'Two summits amongst those in the Alps which yet remained virgin had excited my admiration,' wrote

Whymper at the beginning of the chapter 'My First Scramble on the Matterhorn'.

He was speaking of the Weisshorn and the Matterhorn. Whymper was 'resolved to attempt the ascent of these two peaks without delay'. However, 'rumours were floating about that the former had been conquered and that the latter was shortly to be assailed, and they were confirmed upon arrival at Châtillon, at the entrance of the Val Tournanche'.

The Weisshorn had, in fact, just been climbed, on 19 August, by John Tyndall, with J. J. Bennen and Ulrich Wenger. Therefore that mountain had no further attraction for Whymper.

'My interest in the Weisshorn abated, but it was raised to the highest pitch on hearing that Professor Tyndall was at Breuil, and intending to try to crown his first victory by another and still greater one.'

Thus, from the beginning, Whymper's determination is quite clear to us. From that moment the die was cast; but there were two difficulties which the young Englishman had constantly to face: those arising from the mountain itself, and first and foremost, those arising from the search for a guide who was both competent and strong-minded.

'Up to this time,' Whymper continues, 'my experience with guides had not been fortunate and I was inclined, improperly, to rate them at a low value. They represented to me pointers out of paths, and large consumers of meat and drink, but little more.

'In answer to inquiries at Châtillon, a series of men came forward whose faces expressed malice, pride, envy, hatred, and roguery of every description, but who seemed to be destitute of all good qualities. The arrival of two gentlemen with a guide, who they represented was the embodiment of every virtue, and exactly the man for the Matterhorn, rendered it unnecessary to engage any of the others. He was a man of large proportions; and, although in acquiring him I did not obtain exactly what was wanted, his late employers did exactly what *they* wanted, for I incurred the responsibility, without being aware of it, of paying his back fare, which must have been a relief at once to their minds and to their purses.

'When walking up towards Breuil we inquired for

Jean-Antoine Carrel. From the collection of Paul Payot

43

another man of all the knowing ones, and they, with one voice, proclaimed that Jean-Antoine Carrel, of the village of Valtournanche, was the cock of his valley. We sought, of course, for Carrel; and found him a well-made, resolute-looking fellow, with a certain defiant air which was rather taking. Yes, he would go. Twenty francs a day, whatever was the result, was his price. I assented. But I must take his comrade. "Why so?" Oh, it was impossible to get along without another man. As he said this an evil countenance came forth out of the darkness and proclaimed itself the comrade. I demurred, the negotiations broke off.' Thus from the very first day characters were made clear and problems posed.

Finally Whymper and the guide he had picked up, and whose name he was never to mention, arrived in Breuil on 28 August. Tyndall had just passed through, but had not attempted anything; so the field was clear.

'I had seen the mountain from nearly every direction, and an ascent of it seemed, even to a novice like myself, far too much for one day. I intended to sleep out upon it, as high as possible, and to attempt to reach the summit on the following day. We endeavoured to induce another man to accompany us, but without success. Matthias zum Taugwald and other well-known guides were there at the time, but they declined to go on any account. A sturdy old fellow – Peter Taugwalder by name – said he would go! His price? "Two hundred francs!" "What, whether we ascend or not?" "Yes, nothing less." The end of the matter was, that all the men who were more or less capable showed a strong disinclination, or positively refused to go (their disinclination being very much in proportion to their capacity), or else asked a prohibitive price. This, it may be said, once for all, was the reason why so many futile attempts were made upon the Matterhorn. One first-rate guide after another was brought up to the mountain, and patted on the back, but all declined the business. The men who went had no heart in the matter, and took the first opportunity to turn back. (The guide Bennen must be excepted.) For they were, with the exception of one man, to whom reference will be made presently, universally impressed with the belief that the summit was entirely inaccessible.'

Was it through shortage of guides too, or perhaps for the pleasure of 'going it alone' that in July of that same year, the three brothers Alfred, Charles and Sandbach Parker had made a fresh attempt by way of the Hörnli ridge, and reached a height of about 12,000 feet? 'In neither case did we go as high as we could. At the point where we turned we saw our way for a few hundred feet farther; but, beyond that the difficulties seemed to increase.'

What a pity that the three men did not press on! Anyhow, their attempt was meritorious; they were the first and only climbers to envisage the ascent by way of the Hörnli ridge and to go and study the possibilities on the spot; four years later, it was by this ridge that the first ascent was made.

As for Whymper and his guide, they were to set out alone and spend the night in the highest chalets in the valley.

'The cowherds, good fellows, seldom troubled by tourists, hailed our company with delight,' wrote Whymper, 'and did their best to make us comfortable; brought out their little stores of simple food, and, as we sat with them round the great copper pot which hung over the fire, bade us in husky voice, though with honest intent, to beware of the perils of the haunted cliffs. When night was coming on, we saw, stealing up the hill-side, the forms of Jean-Antoine Carrel and the comrade. "Oh ho!" I said, "you have repented?" "Not at all; you deceive yourself." "Why then have you come here?" "Because we ourselves are going on the mountain tomorrow." "Oh, then it is *not* necessary to have more than three." "Not for *us*." I admired their pluck, and had a strong inclination to engage the pair; but, finally, decided against it. The comrade turned out to be the J. J. Carrel who had been with Mr Hawkins, and was nearly related to the other man.

'Both were bold mountaineers; but Jean-Antoine was incomparably the better man of the two, and was the finest rock-climber I have ever seen. He was the only man who persistently refused to accept defeat, and who continued to believe, in spite of all discouragements, that the great mountain was not inaccessible, and that it could be ascended from the side of his native valley.'

left-hand page
The Matterhorn from Riffelalp. Photo: Pierre Tairraz
pages 46-47
The arrival of bad weather. Photo: Margaret Wunsch

Their night was disturbed only by fleas. The two Carrels left the chalet before dawn. 'We followed them leisurely,' points out Whymper, who did not set out until about seven o'clock, accompanied by the guide he had picked up.

At half past ten, by way of 'a long natural staircase, on which it was seldom necessary to use the hands',

they reached the Col du Lion. 'We decided to pass the night upon the col.' They waited for a while, basked in the sunshine, 'and watched or listened to the Carrels, who were sometimes seen or heard, high above us, upon the ridge leading towards the summit'.

At noon, Whymper and his guide descended to the cow-shed again 'packed up the tent and other properties and returned to the col, although heavily laden, before six o'clock'. It was then that their troubles began again. This tent was constructed on a pattern suggested by Mr Francis Galton, and it was not a success. It looked very pretty when set up in London, but it proved thoroughly useless in the Alps . . . The wind, which playfully careered about the surrounding cliffs, was driven through our gap as through a blow-pipe; the flaps of the tent would not keep down, the pegs would not stay in, and it exhibited so marked a desire to go to the top of the Dent Blanche, that we thought it prudent to take it down and sit upon it.'

The bivouac on the Col de Lion was far from comfortable. Towards midnight there were falls of rock which frightened Whymper and still more his guide, who passed the remainder of the night in a state of shudder'. Promptly at dawn they moved off. An hour later they reached the first tricky passage: 'The Chimney'. 'My companion essayed to go up, and, after crumpling his body into many ridiculous positions, he said that he would not, for he could not, manage it. With some little trouble I got up unassisted, and then my guide tied himself on to the end of our rope, and I endeavoured to pull him up. But he was so awkward that he did little for himself, and so heavy that he proved too much for *me*. After several attempts he untied himself, and quietly observed that he should go down. I told him he was a coward, and *he* mentioned his opinion of *me*. I requested him to go to Breuil, and to say that he had left his "monsieur" on the mountain, and he turned to go; whereupon I had to eat humble pie and ask him to come back; for, although it was not very difficult to go up, and not at all dangerous with a man standing below, it was quite another thing to come down, as the lower edge overhung in a provoking manner.

'The day was perfect; the sun was pouring down grateful warmth; the wind had fallen; the way seemed clear, no insuperable obstacle was in sight; but what could one do alone? I stood on the top, chafing under this unexpected contretemps, and remained for some time irresolute; but as it became apparent that the Chimney was swept more frequently than was necessary (it was a natural channel for falling stones), I turned at last, descended with the assistance of my companion, and returned with him to Breuil, where we arrived about midday.

'The Carrels did not show themselves. We were told that they had not got to any great height.'

The truth was that Jean-Antoine and Jean-Jacques Carrel had climbed that day as far as the arête du Coq, reaching a height of 13,000 feet. A magnificent achievement! It was the first time that such a height had been reached on a ridge of the Matterhorn. Up there,

Jean-Antoine had carved his initials on a slab of rock. 'All his soul,' writes Guido Rey, who knew intimately the inhabitants of Valtournanche, 'is revealed in that action for the first time. It is clear that he had hurried up there to spy on the movements of the man he regarded as an interloper. He was the forward sentry barring the enemy's way. There is no doubt that if Whymper had continued the ascent that day, Carrel would have kept well ahead of him, climbing from one projection to another, already certain, from that moment, of reaching the summit and getting there first – because Carrel saw the Matterhorn as a possession belonging to him by right, and the attempts of others to win it as an encroachment on his own territory. This monstrous jealousy, felt in the impetuous way which was deep in his character, explains clearly his behaviour in the course of the exchanges which followed, and in which it seemed to some people that he had acted in questionable faith; behaviour which was rendered doubtful by his desire to see the Matterhorn mastered and by the egoism which drove him to want the conquest to be reserved for him alone.

Rarely does a powerful and wealthy man feel inclined to credit a poor and ignorant one with an independent will of his own. Those who passed judgment on Carrel did not take into account the fact that though he was uncouth and uneducated, he was by no means servile. He was thought to be born to obey, like so many others, when in fact he was born to command. He was not a man created to promote passively the ambition of another man; he had his own personal ambition; and this, with his confident awareness of his own worth, covered his relations with others like a veil to the end, and denied him the glory of being the first to reach the summit. The Matterhorn exercised the same fascination over Carrel that Mont Blanc had formerly exercised over Jacques Balmat. It was the reason and the aim of his life, and he wanted to climb it from the side of his native valley for the honour of the people of Valtournanche.

He did not see, and he certainly did not wish to believe, that the mountain could be conquered from the opposite side. He lulled himself with the vainglorious illusion that no one would reach the top without him, and he did not hurry. He was beaten to it. No greater pain could have been inflicted upon him.'

No other attempts were made in 1861. Tyndall, in fact, came, but attempted nothing, his guide, J. J. Bennen, having declared to him: 'I have examined the mountain carefully, and I have found it more difficult and dangerous than I thought. There is nowhere fit for us to spend the night. Perhaps we could camp on this snow-covered col, but we would be almost completely frozen there, and in any case quite incapable of attempting the ascent the following day. The rocks offer us no projecting slab or crevice which could give us sufficient shelter; and starting from Breuil it is certainly impossible to reach the summit of the mountain the same day.'

Tyndall was disappointed. Bennen was mistaken, since Carrel and Whymper had bivouacked on the mountain; the true reason was that Bennen despite his desire, was over-awed.

Whymper returned to England, 'longing, more than before, to make the ascent, and determined to return, if possible, with a companion, to lay siege to the mountain until one or the other was vanquished'.

1862

The attempts began very early. T. S. Kennedy thought that the Matterhorn should be less unclimbable in winter than in summer, so he arrived in Zermatt at the beginning of January. Accompanied by Pierre Perrin and Peter Taugwalder, he slept at the chapel at the Schwarzsee. The next day the party climbed nearly 11,000 feet towards the Hörnli ridge, and then returned.

At the beginning of July, Whymper was in Zermatt with Reginald Macdonald, his companion on the Pelvoux. 'Although we failed to secure Melchior Anderegg and some other notable guides, we obtained two men of repute, namely, Johann zum Taugwald and Johann Kronig, of Zermatt.' On the 5th they crossed the Théodule Pass and came down to Breuil to find a porter; the hotel-keeper recommended to them 'a certain Luc Meynet. We found his house a mean abode,'

wrote Whymper, 'encumbered with cheese-making apparatus, and tenanted only by some bright-eyed children; but as they said that uncle Luc would soon be home, we waited at the door of the little chalet and watched for him. At last a speck was seen coming round the corner of the patch of pines below Breuil, and then the children clapped their hands, dropped their toys, and ran eagerly forward to meet him. We saw an ungainly, wobbling figure stoop down and catch up the little ones, kiss them on each cheek, and put them into the empty panniers on each side of the mule, and then heard it come on carolling, as if this was not a world of woe: and yet the face of little Luc Meynet, the hunchback of Breuil, bore traces of trouble and sorrow, and there was more than a touch of sadness in his voice when he said that he must look after his brother's children. All his difficulties were, however, at length overcome, and he agreed to join us to carry the tent.' This time it was a tent of Whymper's own manufacture.

Luc Meynet, tent-bearer.
Drawing by Edward Whymper, photo: Hachette

right-hand page
Whymper's camp on the Col du Lion.
Drawing by Edward Whymper, photo: Hachette

pages 58-59
The Matterhorn seen from Breuil. Photo: Claude Rives

On the morning of July 7th, the party set out. 'I was requested to direct the way,' wrote Whymper, but he took the wrong route; Kronig 'slipped on a streak of ice and went down at a fearful pace'; he 'succeeded in stopping just before he arrived at some rocks that jutted through the snow, which would infallibly have knocked him over'.

They camped on the Col du Lion; during the night a violent wind arose, and in the morning, after having progressed 100 feet, the whole team turned back. 'Complete defeat,' wrote Whymper himself. At least he had two causes for satisfaction: 'Meynet had proved invaluable as a tent-bearer' and 'the tent itself had behaved splendidly'.

At Breuil, Carrel came to hear the news, and 'after some negotiations,' wrote Whymper, 'agreed to accompany us, with one of his friends, named Pession, on the first fine day'.

The wind having dropped during the night, on the morning of the 9th Whymper, Macdonald, Carrel and Pession set off on a fresh attempt. They did not stop on the Col du Lion, Carrel having proposed that they camp higher up. 'We found a protected place; and by building up from ledge to ledge (under the direction of our leader, who at that time was a working mason), we at length constructed a platform of sufficient size and of considerable solidity. Its height was about 12,500 feet above the sea.'

Very early the next morning the team set out, but just when everything had gone so well and the day promised to be a wonderful one misfortune struck. 'At 5.15 we started upwards once more,' wrote Whymper, 'with fine weather and the thermometer at 28°. Carrel scrambled up the Chimney, and Macdonald and I after him. Pession's turn came, but when he arrived at the top he looked very ill, declared himself to be thoroughly incapable, and said that he must go back. We waited some time, but he did not get better, neither could we learn the nature of his illness. Carrel flatly refused to go on with us alone. We were helpless. Macdonald, ever the coolest of the cool, suggested that we should try what we could do without them; but our better judgment prevailed, and, finally, we returned together to Breuil.'

Whymper then summed up his attempts:

'Three times I had essayed the ascent of this mountain, and on each occasion had failed ignominiously. I had

not advanced a yard beyond my predecessors. Up to the height of nearly 13,000 feet there were no extraordinary difficulties; the way so far, might even become "a matter of amusement". Only 1,800 feet remained; but they were as yet untrodden, and might present the most formidable obstacles. No man could expect to climb them by himself. A morsel of rock only seven feet high might at any time defeat him, if it were perpendicular. Such a place might be possible to two, or a bagatelle to three men. It was evident that a party should consist of three men at least. But where could the other two men be obtained? Carrel was the only man who exhibited any enthusiasm in the matter; and he, in 1861, had absolutely refused to go unless the party consisted of at least *four* persons. Want of men made the difficulty, not the mountain.'

Whymper then went to Zermatt, 'on the chance of picking up a man', but in vain: 'Not one of the better men, however, could be induced to come, and I returned to Breuil on the 17th, hoping to combine the skill of Carrel with the willingness of Meynet on a new attempt, by the same route as before; for the upper part of the north-eastern ridge, which I had inspected in the meantime, seemed to be entirely impracticable. Both men were inclined to go, but their ordinary occupations prevented them from starting at once.' They were not guides by profession.

While waiting for Carrel and Meynet to become available, Whymper set off again for the Matterhorn. 'My tent had been left rolled up at the second platform,' he wrote, 'and whilst waiting for the men it occurred to me that it might have been blown away during the late stormy weather.' So on the 18th he started out alone 'because no man was available' to see what had become of it. 'The tent was safe, although snowed up.' Reassured, Whymper contemplated for a moment the extraordinary landscape that lay about him; then he decided not to return to Breuil, but to spend the night where he was. 'As I sat at the door of the tent, and watched the twilight change to darkness, the earth seemed to become less earthy and almost sublime; the world seemed dead, and I, its sole inhabitant.' The following day, in splendid

weather, Whymper continued his climb in search of another and higher spot to pitch his tent.

Alone, and therefore doubly cautious, he reached the foot of the Grande Tour, 'which,' he wrote, 'stands out like a turret at the angle of a castle. Behind it a battlemented wall leads upwards to the citadel. Seen from the Théodule pass it looks only an insignificant pinnacle, but as one approaches it (on the ridge) so it seems to rise, and, when one is at its base, it completely conceals the upper parts of the mountain'.

Whymper found 'a suitable place for the tent; which, although not so well protected as the second platform, possessed the advantage of being 300 feet higher up'. Then he continued his climb, and encountered serious difficulties. ''Tis vain to attempt to describe such places. Whether they are sketched with a light hand, or wrought out in laborious detail, one stands an equal chance of being misunderstood. Their enchantment to the climber arises from their calls on his faculties, in their demands on his strength, and on overcoming the impediments which they oppose to his skill.'

Whymper climbed as far as the strip of snow which had been christened 'the Cravate'; that is to say, to 13,260 feet. 'My neighbour, the Dent d'Hérens, still rose above me,' he wrote, 'although but slightly, and the height which had been attained could be measured by its help. So far, I had no doubts about my capacity to descend that which had been ascended; but, in a short time, on looking ahead, I saw that the cliffs steepened, and I turned back (without pushing on to them, and getting into inextricable difficulties), exulting in the thought that they would be passed when we returned together, and that I had, without assistance, got nearly to the height of the Dent d'Hérens, and considerably higher than anyone had been before.'

Towards five in the evening Whymper left his tent and continued the descent. Below the Col du Lion he suddenly slipped on the ice, the weight of his rucksack dragged him backwards, he fell against some rocks which flung him head-first back into the gully, and, in seven or eight rebounds which sent him from one side of the gully to the other, he cleared 200 feet at break-neck speed. Finally, he stopped on the edge of the precipice: 'Ten feet more would have taken me in one gigantic leap of 800 feet on to the glacier below.'

After such a fall, he was severely bruised, but by a

miracle he had no bones broken. For a moment he was unconscious; then he came round. He continued his descent, and with great courage reached Breuil. 'I entered the inn stealthily, wishing to escape to my room unnoticed. But Favre met me in the passage, demanded "Who is it?" screamed with fright when he got a light, and aroused the household. Two dozen heads then held solemn council over mine, with more talk than action. The natives were unanimous in recommending that hot wine mixed with salt should be rubbed into the cuts. I protested, but they insisted. It was all the doctoring they received. Whether their rapid healing was to be attributed to that simple remedy, or to a good state of health, is a question. They closed up remarkably quickly, and in a few days I was able to move again.'

The news of the accident brought J.-A. Carrel running up, 'and along with the haughty chasseur came one of his relatives, a strong and able young fellow named César. With these two men and Meynet I made another start on the 23rd of July', wrote Whymper.

They reached the tent without difficulty. The following day they continued the ascent, got beyond the Tour, and were scaling the rocks above it, when quite suddenly the weather broke. 'In a few minutes snow fell heavily. We stopped, as this part was exceedingly difficult, and, unwilling to retreat, remained on the spot several hours, in hopes that another change would occur; but, as it did not, we at length went down to the base of the Great Tower, and commenced to make a third platform, at the height of 12,992 feet above the sea. It still continued to snow, and we took refuge in the tent.'

Whymper would have preferred to wait, but Carrel thought the bad weather was going to last, and finally they turned back.

'Carrel was not an easy man to manage. He was perfectly aware that he was the cock of the Val Tournanche, and he commanded the other men as by right. He was equally conscious that he was indispensable to me, and took no pains to conceal his knowledge of the fact. If he had been commanded, or if he had been entreated to stop, it would have been all the same. But, let me repeat, he was the only first-class climber I could find who believed that the mountain was not inaccessible. With him I had hopes, but without him none; so he was allowed to do as he would. His will on this occasion was almost incomprehensible. He certainly could not be charged with cowardice, for a bolder man could hardly be found; nor was he turning away on account of difficulty, for nothing to which we had yet come seemed to be difficult to *him*; and his strong personal desire to make the ascent was evident. There was no occasion to come down on account of food, for we had taken, to guard against this very casualty, enough to last for a week; and there was no danger, and little or no discomfort, in stopping in the tent. It seemed to me that he was spinning out the ascent for his own purposes, and that although he wished very much to be the first man on the top, and did not object to be accompanied by anyone else who had the same wish, he had no intention of letting one succeed too soon–perhaps to give a greater appearance of *éclat* when the thing was accomplished. As he feared no rival, he may have supposed that the more difficulties he made the more valuable he would be estimated; though, to do him justice, he never showed any great hunger for money. His demands were fair, not excessive; but he always stipulated for so much per day, and so, under any circumstances, he did not do badly.

'Vexed at having my time thus frittered away, I was still well pleased when he volunteered to start again on the morrow, if it was fine. We were to advance the tent to the foot of the Tower, to fix ropes in the most difficult parts beyond, and to make a push for the summit on the following day.'

The following morning Whymper sought out Luc Meynet again, but the two Carrels were not there: they had notified Meynet 'that they intended marmot-hunting, as the day was favourable for that sport'.

'As a last resort,' Whymper went on, 'I proposed to the hunchback to accompany me alone, to see if we could not get higher than before, though of reaching the summit there was little or no hope.' I find that, and Meynet's affirmative answer, extremely engaging: 'He did not hesitate,' wrote Whymper, 'and in a few hours

we stood—for the third time together—upon the Col du Lion.' An odd team, consisting of the tall, rather ungainly Englishman and the little hunchback, on the formidable mountain!

'It was the first time Meynet had seen the view unclouded. The poor little deformed peasant gazed upon it silently and reverently for a time, and then, unconsciously, fell on one knee in an attitude of adoration, and clasped his hands, exclaiming in ecstasy, "Oh, beautiful mountains!" His actions were as appropriate as his words were natural, and tears bore witness to the reality of his emotion.'

The two climbers bivouacked on the col; very early next morning they resumed the climb, and their manly courage and tenacity were rewarded, for they went higher than anyone had ever been, reaching an altitude of 13,325 feet. 'At length we were both spread-eagled on the all but perpendicular face, unable to advance, and barely able to descend. We returned to the ridge. It was almost equally difficult, and infinitely more unstable; and at length, after having pushed our attempts as far as was prudent, I determined to return to Breuil, and to have a light ladder made to assist us to overcome some of the steepest parts.'

During the descent, which was very swift, Whymper and Meynet stopped only once, at the very beginning, 250 feet below the point they had reached, in order to carve their names on the slab on which J.-A. Carrel had carved his the year before.

Thus they returned from the young Englishman's fifth attempt since his arrival in Breuil; no one had shown so much perseverance or obtained better results: six days earlier, alone, he had climbed higher than anyone else; today, with the little hunchback, he had further improved this record; where would he have got to with a robust and determined companion? He hoped that Carrel 'by this time would have had enough marmot-hunting, and would deign to accompany us again'. So everything was ready for a decisive assault! He could therefore be tolerant about the previous day's hitch: his day had not been completely wasted; it had confirmed his resolve, and he was full of hope when he reached the inn at Breuil.

'I found my projects,' wrote Whymper, 'summarily and unexpectedly knocked on the head.'

Accompanied by the guides Johan Joseph Bennen and Anton Walter, Professor Tyndall had arrived in Breuil during Whymper's short absence and engaged Jean-Antoine and César Carrel as porters. The ladder and provisions were ready. Their departure was fixed for the following morning.

Whymper was astonished and at first failed to understand: a year earlier, after carefully surveying the Matterhorn, Bennen had declared it unclimbable and judged any attempt doomed to failure.

'It was useless to compete with the Professor and his four men, who were ready to start in a few hours, so I waited to see what would come of their attempt. Everything seemed to favour it,' wrote Whymper.

'They set out on a fine morning in high spirits, leaving me tormented with envy and all uncharitableness. If they succeeded, they carried off the prize for which I had been so long struggling; and if they failed, there was no time to make another attempt, for I was due in a few days more in London,' he added.

In fact, before this, an uncomfortable conversation had taken place between Tyndall and Whymper. 'Arrived at Breuil,' wrote Tyndall, 'we found that a gentleman whose long perseverance merited victory was then upon the mountain.' And he added: 'At night, Mr Whymper returned from the Matterhorn, having left his tent upon the rocks. In the frankest spirit, he placed it at my disposal.'

For his part Whymper states precisely: 'As the Professor was ready to start, it would have been useless to compete with him. My tent was on the mountain, at a height of about 12,500 feet, and it seems to me that I should have been lacking in courtesy if I had not placed it at his disposal, for if I had not, he would have been obliged either to bivouac lower down, or to move it, or to use it without permission, or to make a new platform for himself higher up.'

Tyndall went on: 'The presence of Mr Whymper, if he should have been able to accompany me, would doubtless have added to the pleasure of the excursion; his whole heart was in this struggle with the Matterhorn and it was my keenest desire that he should not be disappointed in his hopes.' And then, perhaps through weakness or duplicity, Tyndall added: 'I consulted Bennen who had heard many stories, probably exaggerated, of Mr Whymper's prowess. He shook his head, but in the end agreed that Mr Whymper should be invited

"on condition that he showed himself to be reasonable".
I therefore asked Mr Whymper to join us. His reply was:
"If I go on to the Matterhorn, I must be the one to
lead." ' 'In view of my own experience at that time,'
Tyndall went on, 'and above all, considering the
reputation and the ability of my guide, I regarded this
reply as being anything but "reasonable" and so I set
off alone.'

Certainly, Tyndall, who had just climbed the Weisshorn, could claim greater general experience, but
Whymper had far more experience of the Matterhorn
itself, and this was allied with a degree of will-power and
physical strength which was quite uncommon.

'I entirely agree with Professor Tyndall,' answered
Whymper, 'that such a reply to his counter offer would
have been the opposite of good sense. However, my
recollection of this conversation is very different from his.
I absolutely deny having given such a reply, and I affirm
no less positively that my response was in no way
intended to have the meaning which he gives it.' This
seems plausible, and even obvious, for Whymper, not
wanting to let any chance slip, wished to be included
in the party. Here is his explanation: 'About an hour
after he had accepted my offer (concerning the tent), he
came to me and (in a manner which, I thought, seemed
to imply that the reply should not be in the affirmative)
said: "Mr Whymper, would you not like to accompany
us?" My response could not have left him in the least
doubt, for I replied with some warmth: "Certainly, I
should like to. That is all I ask for," or words to that
effect. Professor Tyndall then went on: "If you come
with us you must put yourself under Bennen's orders;
you must obey his instructions, and follow him wherever
he goes," and more like that. Naturally I was quite
prepared to place myself under Bennen's orders, and I
would have done so, that goes without saying, if I had
accompanied the party. But before saying that I would
obey his instructions implicitly, whether they were good
or bad, I could not help saying: "Remember, Dr
Tyndall, that I have climbed much higher than Bennen
and that I have stayed eleven days on the mountain
whereas he has not spent a single day there. You nevertheless expect me to follow him even if he is obviously
mistaken." ' It seems to me quite fair to acknowledge
the honesty and frankness of Whymper, who goes on:
'So much time has passed since then that I cannot recall

the exact words that were spoken, but those suggested
above cannot be far from the truth. Whatever was said,
it was said because I wanted the expedition to succeed,
and I thought that Dr Tyndall had understood me
perfectly, for our conversation was not interrupted; it
was agreed that I should accompany the party and I
went to my room to make preparations to this end.
Shortly after this, perhaps half an hour or more, Dr
Tyndall came to me and said: "I think, after all, it
would be better if you did not come with us." He gave
no reason to justify this change of attitude and I did not
ask him for one. I just supposed that he wanted to be
alone.' To tell the truth, Whymper was so strong and
determined that he repelled everyone, and especially
those who were not sure of themselves.

Whymper would have preferred to decide to return
to London as planned, but he did not manage to do so:

The guide J. J. Bennen. Drawing by Edward Whymper,
photo: Hachette

pages 68-69
Upper section of the Matterhorn seen from the
south-west; centre, the Lion arête; left, west face and
Zmutt ridge; right, south face with, top right, the
Furggen arête. Photo: Bradford Washburn

'I resolved to leave Breuil at once, but, when packing up, found that some necessaries had been left behind in the tent. So I went off about midday to recover them.'

Whymper overtook Professor Tyndall's party 'as they were going very slowly' when they were about to reach the Col du Lion, and stopped for lunch there. Then he carried on as far as the third platform at about 12,642 feet.

'I waited at the tent to welcome the Professor, and when he arrived went down to Breuil.'

Whether they were English, like Whymper and Tyndall; Swiss, like Bennen; or Italian, like Carrel; these men were tough, frightfully tough.

'Early next morning,' writes Whymper, 'someone ran to me saying that a flag was seen on the summit of the Matterhorn. It was not so, however, although I saw that they had passed the place where we had turned back on the 26th. I had now no doubt of their final success, for they had got beyond the point which Carrel, not less than myself, had always considered to be the most questionable place on the whole mountain.'

'My knapsack was packed,' Whymper continues, 'but I could not bring myself to leave until the result was heard, and lingered about, as a foolish lover hovers round the object of his affections, even after he has been contemptuously rejected. The sun had set before the men were descried coming over the pastures. There was no spring in their steps – they, too, were defeated. The Carrels hid their heads, and the others said, as men will do when they have been beaten, that the mountain was horrible, impossible, and so forth. Professor Tyndall told me they had arrived *within a stone's throw of the summit*, and admonished me to have nothing more to do with the mountain. I understood him to say that he should not try again, and ran down to the village of Valtournanche, almost inclined to believe that the mountain was inaccessible, leaving the tent, ropes and other matters in the hands of Favre, to be placed at the disposal of any person who wished to ascend it, more, I am afraid, out of irony than for generosity.'

What, in fact, had happened up there? Professor Tyndall's party had reached the south-west shoulder of the Matterhorn, but had subsequently been unable to cross the quite deep and above all awe-inspiring chasm that separated it from the pyramid of the summit. It was on the edges of this chasm, which came to be called the 'Enjambée' that the game was played out, and there again, of course, there are different and even contradictory versions: 'There are material discrepancies between the published narratives of Professor Tyndall and the verbal accounts of the Carrels.'

'The ridge,' writes Professor Tyndall, 'was here split by a deep cleft which separated it from the final precipice, and the case became more hopeless as we came more near. We had never before found ourselves in such a wild place. We sat down, our hopes fled.'

'Tyndall's party,' writes Whymper, 'after arriving at "the Shoulder" was led by his guides along the crest of the ridge, and, consequently, when they got to its northern end, they came to the top of the notch, instead of the bottom – to the dismay of all but the Carrels.'

'This notch,' adds Whymper, 'was not unknown to me, as I had seen it from afar, long before Professor Tyndall's party arrived there. One can see it very well from the Théodule Pass side and I had often discussed with Carrel the best way of getting over it. Carrel knew perfectly well of its existence – he knew of it, in truth, some years before I did. But Professor Tyndall, Bennen and Walter seem not have seen it before having been stopped by it. Bennen, the guide who led the team, did not succeed in finding a place where they could pass. Tyndall called to the others to get him out of his difficulties. But they did not respond. According to the Professor they all declared that any progress was impossible. As far as he was concerned, J.-A. Carrel would have nothing to do with it, and César Carrel too, and when Tyndall asked them for their opinion they replied: "We were engaged as *porters*, ask your guides".

'When it became clear that Bennen could not go any further, Tyndall gave the order to turn back. At this moment, Jean-Antoine was tempted to advance a few steps to examine the route, but the Professor told him to follow Bennen, which he was naturally obliged to do and to return.'

The exploration of the Matterhorn had progressed, but victory was still far off.

1863

On July 29th, Wymper crossed the Channel and arrived in France loaded with two ladders, each 15 feet long and capable of being joined like those used by firemen.

'My luggage was highly suggestive of house-breaking, for besides these, there were several coils of rope, and numerous tools of suspicious appearance, and it was reluctantly admitted into France, but it passed through the custom-house with less trouble than I anticipated, after a timely expenditure of a few francs.'

His troubles began again at Susa as he entered Italy. 'The officials there, more honest and more obtuse than the Frenchmen, declined at one and the same time to be bribed, or to pass my baggage until a satisfactory account of it was rendered; and, as they refused to believe the true explanation, I was puzzled what to say, but was presently relieved from the dilemma by one of the men, who was cleverer than his fellows, suggesting that I was going to Turin to perform in the streets; that I mounted the ladder and balanced myself on the end of it, then lighted my pipe and put the point of the bâton in its bowl, and caused the bâton to gyrate around my head. The rope was to keep back the spectators, and an Englishman in my company was the agent. "Monsieur is an acrobat then?" "Yes, certainly." "Pass the effects of Monsieur the acrobat." '

Finally, Whymper arrived in Breuil on July 31st. The next day Carrel was ready to go with him, but it was raining, and because of the fresh snow the heights of the Matterhorn would be inaccessible for several days. Whymper and Carrel passed the time by making a circuit of the Matterhorn together in order to examine the famous pyramid on all sides. On Monday, 10 August, the clouds having dispersed at last, they set out. The team was composed of Whymper, J.-A. Carrel, César Carrel, Luc Meynet and two porters.

They reached the col at nine o'clock. 'Already we had found that the bad weather of the past week had done its work. The rocks for several hundred feet below the col were varnished with ice. Loose, incoherent snow covered the older and harder beds below, and we nearly lost our leader through its treacherousness. He stepped on some snow which seemed firm, and raised his axe to deliver a swinging blow, but, just as it was highest, the crust of the slope upon which he stood broke away, and poured down in serpentine streams, leaving long, bare strips, which glittered in the sun, for they were glassy ice. Carrel, with admirable readiness, flung

himself back on to the rock off which he had stepped, and was at once secured. He simply remarked, "It is time we were tied up," and, after we had been tied up, he went to work again as if nothing had happened.'

Whymper goes on: 'We had abundant illustrations during the next two hours of the value of a rope to climbers . . . For these rocks (which, it has been already said, were easy enough under ordinary circumstances) were now difficult in a high degree . . . The weather was superb, the men made light of the toil, and shouted to rouse the echoes from the Dent d'Hérens.

'We went on gaily, passed the second tent platform, the Chimney, and the other well-remembered points, and reckoned confidently on sleeping that night upon

John Tyndall. From the collection of Emile Gos

page 72
A storm at the Grande Tour (10 August 1863).
Drawing by Edward Whymper, photo: Hachette

page 73
The Grande Tour on the Lion arête. Photo: Alfonso Bernardi

pages 74-75
Tête du Cervin: on the right, the Lion Arête; facing, the west side; on the left, the Zmutt ridge.
Photo: Bradford Washburn

the top of "the Shoulder", but, before we had well arrived at the foot of the Great Tower, a sudden rush of cold air warned us to look out.'

It is only fair to acknowledge that Whymper, whose willpower was at once admirable and extraordinary, was out of luck once more. 'Before we could take off our packs, and get under any kind of shelter, a hurricane of snow burst upon us from the east. It fell very heavily, and in a few minutes the ridge was covered by it. "What shall we do?" I shouted to Carrel. "Monsieur," said he, "the wind is bad; the weather has changed; we are heavily laden. Here is a fine gîte; let us stop! If we go on we shall be half-frozen. That is *my* opinion." No one differed from him; so we fell to work to make a place for the tent, and in a couple of hours completed the platform which we had commenced in 1862. The clouds had blackened during that time, and we had hardly finished our task before a thunderstorm broke upon us with appalling fury. Forked lightning shot out at the turrets above, and at the crag below. It was so close that we quailed at its darts. It seemed to scorch us—we were in the very focus of the storm.'

It seems that misfortune heaped upon misfortune overwhelmed Whymper that day: 'The bad weather was evidently confined to the Matterhorn, for when the clouds lifted we could see everything that could be seen from our gîte. Monte Viso, a hundred miles off, was clear, and the sun set gorgeously behind the range of Mont Blanc. We passed the night comfortably—even luxuriously—in our blanket-bags, but there was little chance of sleeping, between the noise of the wind, of the thunder, and of the falling rocks. I forgave the thunder for the sake of the lightning. A more splendid spectacle than its illumination of the Matterhorn crags I do not expect to see.'

On the 11th, the team rose at three-thirty in the morning; it was still snowing. It was not until nine o'clock that the snow ceased and a very feeble sun showed itself. The climbers started out to try to reach the Shoulder. They climbed with great difficulty until it began to snow again; it was eleven o'clock.

'We held a council; the opinions expressed at it were unanimous against advancing, and I decided to retreat.'

The team descended to Breuil. 'It was quite fine there,' writes Whymper, 'and the tenants of the inn received our statements with evident scepticism. They were astonished to learn that we had been exposed to a snow-storm of twenty-six hours' duration.'

The same day, at midnight, Whymper arrived at Châtillon, 'defeated and disconsolate; but like a gambler who loses each throw,' he adds, 'only the more eager to have another try, to see if the luck would change; and returned to London ready to devise fresh combinations, and to form new plans'.

1864

1864 was a year of truce on the Matterhorn.

Whymper made the first crossing of the Brèche de la Meije, the first ascent of the Barre des Écrins, the first crossing of the Col de la Pilatte, the first ascent of Mont Dolen, the Aiguille de Trélatête and the Aiguille d'Argentière. This, in a few days was an exceptional list of conquests, but most important of all, Whymper had made the acquaintance of a guide of the first rank, Michel-Auguste Croz.

'Michel Croz had been engaged in both of these expeditions in Dauphiné,' writes Whymper, 'and I naturally looked to him for assistance. Mr Mathews (to whom I applied for information) gave him a high character, and concluded his reply to me by saying that Croz "was only happy when upwards of 10,000 feet high".

'I know what my friend meant. Croz was happiest when he was employing his powers to the utmost. Places where you and I would "toil and sweat, and yet be freezing cold", were bagatelles to him, and it was only when he got above the range of ordinary mortals, and was required to employ his magnificent strength, and to draw upon his unsurpassed knowledge of ice and snow, that he could be said to be really and truly happy.

'Of all the guides with whom I travelled, Michel Croz was the man who was most after my own heart. He did not work like a blunt razor, and take to his toil

unkindly. He did not need urging, or to be told a second time to do anything. You had only to say *what* was to be done, and *how* it was to be done, and the work *was* done, if it was possible. Such men are not common, and when they are known they are valued. Michel was not widely known, but those who did know him came again and again. The inscription that is placed upon his tomb truthfully records that he was "beloved by his comrades and esteemed by travellers".'

Michel Croz was born on 22 April 1830, in the village of Le Tour, in the upper valley of Chamonix. The first thirty years of his life passed unsensationally. He worked as a porter and sometimes as a guide. He lived with his brother Jean-Baptiste, his two sisters and other relations. He wished to dedicate his life to the mountains; he did not marry. It seems that he was awaiting his chance as a mountaineer. It came in 1859, when, in mid-season, Mr William Mathews engaged him to make the ascent of Mont Blanc. Mathews noticed his skill immediately, and before leaving the valley he retained him for the following year.

1860 marks the beginning of Croz's true career; for five years he was to accompany the best amateurs of the period on the greatest expeditions, and often on the finest first ascents. First with Mathews, Bonney and Hawkins, then with Tuckett, Moore, Adams-Reilly and above all Whymper, he was to spend the best moments of his short life. Great amateurs had found a great guide: his idea of happiness was to guide them wherever they wished.

In 1861, with Mathews, he made the first ascent of Monte Viso; in 1862 he made the first crossing of the Col des Écrins, the Col du Sélé and the Col du Glacier Blanc with Tuckett, Pierre Perren and Bartolomeo Peyrotte. In 1863 he climbed the Grandes Rousses with Mathews, T. G. Bonney and his brother Jean-Baptiste Croz. Finally, in the following year he achieved a considerable number of first ascents: the crossing of the Brèche de la Meije, the ascent of the Barre des Écrins, the crossing of the Col de la Pilatte with Whymper, Horace Walker, A. W. Moore and Christian Almer.

Incapable of jealousy, Croz experienced real pleasure in working with the great guide from the Oberland. 'The combination of Croz and Almer was a perfect one,' declares Whymper. 'Both men were in the prime of life; both were endued with strength and activity far beyond the average; and the courage and knowledge of each was alike undoubted. The temper of Almer it was impossible to ruffle; he was ever obliging and enduring a bold but a safe man. That which he lacked in fire—in dash—was supplied by Croz, who, in his turn, was kept in place by Almer. It is pleasant to remember how they worked together, and how each one confided to you that he "liked the other *so* much because he worked *so* well".'

'Just below the summit of the Écrins, Almer was a few feet in front, and he, with characteristic modesty, hesitated to step on the highest point, and drew back to allow us to pass. A cry was raised for Croz, who had done the chief part of the work, but he declined the honour, and we marched on to the top simultaneously.' All this is so likeable, and admirably reflects the spirit of the rope-team. Some great first ascents were certainly achieved, technique was invented and then perfected, it was the golden age of alpinism, but foremost was the extraordinary atmosphere of these great triumphs.

Having descended from the Col de la Pilatte, Whymper writes again: 'I cannot close this chapter without paying tribute to the ability with which Croz led us, through a dense mist, down the remainder of the Glacier de la Pilatte. As an exhibition of strength and skill, it has seldom been surpassed in the Alps or elsewhere.'

In the same year, still early in the season, Croz, assisted by Michel Payot, guided Whymper and Adams-Reilly to the Col du Triolet on July 8th, to Mont Dolent on the 9th, to the Aiguille de Trélatête on the 12th and to the Aiguille d'Argentière on the 15th—all first ascents. Finally, on July 18th, Croz and Whymper who had joined up with Christian Almer and A. W. Moore again at Zinal, were to achieve the first crossing of the Moming Pass in very difficult conditions.

Whymper writes: 'Croz displayed the most admirable courage in getting us out of the frightful danger which threatened us; not for a moment did he take his eyes off the work he had to do. He glanced neither to the right nor the left.' Farther on, when they arrived at the Pass, an immense cornice, 'like a wave, which the cold had

The Matterhorn in winter. Photo: Heimhuber

frozen upon the ocean at the very moment it was about to fall' overhung the Zermatt face.

'Croz,' Whymper goes on '–held hard in by the others, who kept down the Zinal side–opened his shoulders, flogged down the foam, and cut away the cornice to its junction with the summit; then boldly leaped down, and called on us to follow him.

'It was well for us now that we had such a man as leader. An inferior or less daring guide would have hesitated to enter upon the descent in a dense mist; and Croz himself would have done right to pause had he been less magnificent in physique. He acted, rather than said, "Where snow lies fast, there man can go; where ice exists, a way may be cut; it is a question of power; I have the power–all you have to do is to follow me." Truly, he did not spare himself, and could he have performed the feats upon the boards of a theatre that he did upon this occasion, he would have brought down the house with thunders of applause.'

Croz and Whymper in bivouac.
Drawing by Edward Whymper, photo: Hachette

right-hand page
Michel-Auguste Croz. From the collection of Emile Gos

At twenty past seven in the evening the party reached Zermatt and went to the Monte Rosa Hotel, the usual meeting place of climbers and guides. 'I left this agreeable society,' writes Whymper, 'to seek letters at the post. They yielded disastrous intelligence, and my holiday was brought to an abrupt termination.' He had been unexpectedly recalled to London.

So there was no attempt on the Matterhorn. 1864 was a year of truce, but not a wasted year: Whymper had met Michel Croz, who was to be the key-man of the ascent.

1865

Every mountain has its great year; for Mont Blanc it was 1786, for the Matterhorn, 1865. These two dates are in themselves more significant than the two mountains–one of snow, the other of rock–each in its way as famous as it is supremely beautiful, for between these two dates is inscribed the golden age of alpinism.

Whymper had halted a programme which was 'rather ambitious, since it included almost all of the great peaks which had not then been ascended'; and, of course, he was more determined than ever to climb the Matterhorn. He had studied the defeats of others, 'that their errors might be avoided', and had prepared his alpine campaign with extreme care–so much so that in his accounts he was able to say: 'Most of our ascents were made upon the very days which had been fixed for them months beforehand . . . up to a certain point, the programme was completely and happily carried out.' An unfortunate omission to confirm Croz's engagement was to be the indirect cause of a terrible catastrophe.

On June 13th, more determined and more impatient than ever, Whymper was already in the Alps; on the 14th he crossed the Petersgrat with Christian Almer and Johann Tännler to reach Tourtemagne in the Valais, where he rejoined Michel Croz and Franz Biener. On the 15th they reached Zinal by way of the Col de la Forcletta. On the 16th they made the first ascent of the Grand Cornier. On the 17th they intended to cross the Col d'Hérens to reach Zermatt, but on the way Whymper put the following question to his guides: 'Which is best for us to do?–to ascend the Dent Blanche, or to cross to Zermatt?' They answered, with befitting solemnity,

'We think Dent Blanche is best.' What a marvellous era it was!

A 'diabolical' wind rose, and the bad weather became a factor seriously to be reckoned with. The party continued the ascent. Yet, to tell the truth, the Dent Blanche was hardly more than an exercise. Whymper's mind was not on it, but on the mountain opposite: 'My old enemy—the Matterhorn—seen across the basin of the Z'Mutt Glacier, looked totally unassailable. "Do you think," the men asked, "that you or anyone else, will ever get up *that* mountain?" And when, undismayed by their ridicule, I stoutly answered, "Yes, but not upon that side," they burst into derisive chuckles. I must confess that my hopes sank; for nothing can look more completely inaccessible than the Matterhorn on its northern and north-west sides.' Meanwhile the cold and the wind became terrible. They reached the summit, and found a cairn there. Immediately they turned and began the descent: 'The men looked like impersonations of winter, with their hair all frosted, and their beards matted with ice . . . If they had worked less vigorously, or harmoniously, we should have been benighted upon the face, where there was not a single spot upon which it was possible to sit; and if that had happened, I do not think that one would have survived to tell the tale.'

The next day the party tried to cross the Col d'Hérens but turned back because of the very heavy mist, and it was only on the following day, the 19th, that they crossed the col and reached Zermatt. Without wasting a day, they crossed the Théodule Pass on the 20th, climbing the Théodulhorn on the way, 'so as to examine' Whymper says precisely, 'a new route I had devised to the Matterhorn'. He had in fact decided to give up the Italian ridge to try the Swiss ridge. However, Almer and Biener refused point-blank to attempt the ascent from that side. Thereupon Whymper suggested a hybrid route, passing first by way of the south side and then by way of the east side.

The party descended to Breuil. 'Luc Meynet, the gallant little hunchback, summoned to the hotel, declared himself very happy to take up again his old job of tent-bearer. Favre's *cuisine* hastened to prepare rations for three days'; and, although they had arrived only in the evening, the party set off again at 5.45 the following morning, taking the road to Breuiljoch, which they left after three hours' march to make for a gully, the beginning of the route advocated by Whymper. 'The nearer we got, the more favourable did it seem. However, we observed at its base some evidence that made us fear avalanches of stones.' At ten o'clock, at a suitable place for a halt, the party stopped. While the guides were preparing the lunch, Whymper went on a short distance to survey the way ahead, and to study a bend in the gully about a thousand feet higher up. Then, suddenly 'falling at a speed of forty-five miles an hour, a stone came down, followed by many others'. 'I did not warn the guides,' Whymper adds. 'I was unwilling to alarm the men unnecessarily, and said nothing. They did not hear the stones. Almer was seated on a rock, carving large slices from a leg of mutton, the others were chatting and the first intimation they had of danger was from a crash—a sudden roar—which reverberated awfully amongst the cliffs, and, looking up, they saw masses of rocks, boulders and stones, big and little, dart round the corner 800 feet or so above us, fly with fearful fury against the opposite cliffs, rebound from them against the walls on our side, and descend; some ricocheting from side to side in a frantic manner; some bounding down in leaps of a hundred feet or more over the snow, and others trailing down in a jumbled, confused mass mixed with snow and ice, deepening the grooves which, a moment before, had excited my admiration.

'The men looked wildly around for protection, and dropping the food, dashed under cover in all directions.

left-hand page
Zermatt and the Matterhorn. From the collection of Paul Payot

pages 86-87
The Monte Rosa Hotel at Zermatt. From left to right
Group I: F. Crawford Grove (with bowler hat), Leslie Stephen (sitting sideways), George E. Foster (standing behind him), Frank Walker (soft hat), the Rev. J Robertson (standing, without beard), A. W. Moore (seated, leaning forward), Reginald S. Macdonald (sitting astride his chair).
Group II: John Ball (standing in the foreground, rope across chest), William Mathews, T. S. Kennedy, T. G. Bonney, John Tyndall, Ulrich Lauener (behind, ice-axe on shoulder), Alfred Wills (arms folded)
Group III: Miss Lucy Walker, Franz Andermatten (seated with rope) Joseph Maquignaz (standing, smoking), Peter Taugwalder junior (seated, with bowler hat).
Pierre Perren (standing, extreme right)
Drawing by Edward Whymper, photo: Hachette

The precious mutton was pitched on one side, the wine-bag was let fall, and its contents gushed out from the unclosed neck, whilst all four cowered under defending rocks, endeavouring to make themselves as small as possible. Let it not be supposed that their fright was unreasonable, or that I was free from it.' Whymper goes on. 'I took good care to make myself safe, and went and cringed in a cleft until the storm had passed. But their scramble to get under shelter was indescribably ludicrous. Such a panic I have never witnessed, before or since, upon a mountainside . . . . Thus my little plan was knocked on the head, and we were thrown back upon the original scheme'

The party regained the Breuiljoch; Whymper intended to make for the Hörnli to attack the east side of the Matterhorn, but the descent of the Furggen glacier turned out to be impracticable, heavy clouds were coming from all directions and the wind began to blow fiercely. The guides had little enthusiasm for carrying on. Whymper writes: 'Almer asked, with more point than politeness, "Why don't you try to go up a mountain which *can* be ascended?" "It is impossible," chimed in Biener. "Sir," said Croz, "if we cross to the other side we shall lose three days, and very likely shall not succeed. You want to make ascents in the chain of Mont Blanc, and I believe they can be made. But I shall not be able to make them with you if I spend these days here, for I must be at Chamonix on the 27th"'

Snow began to fall. That settled the question. The party descended to Breuil, and from there to Châtillon, to get back to Courmayeur

'I cannot but regret that the counsels of the guides prevailed,' Whymper continues. 'If Croz had not uttered his well-intentioned words, he might still have been living. He parted from us at Chamonix at the appointed time, but by a strange chance we met again at Zermatt three weeks later, and two days afterwards he perished before my eyes on the very mountain from which we turned away, at his advice, on the 21st June.'

On June 25th, 'under the dexterous leading of Michel Croz', they climbed the Grandes Jorasses

On June 27th the team made the first passage of the Col Dolent; the descent of the very steep and completely ice-covered north face was an extraordinary exploit

'Michel Croz now parted from us,' writes Whymper.

'His new employer had not arrived at Chamonix, but Croz considered he was bound by honour to wait for him . . . .'

The previous year, before returning to England, Whymper had retained Croz for the following summer. ' . . . upon writing to him in the month of April to fix the dates of his engagement, I found that he had supposed he was free (in consequence of not having heard from me earlier), and had engaged himself to a Mr B—from the 27th of June. I endeavoured to hold him to his promise, but he considered himself unable to withdraw from his later obligation. His letters were honourable to him. The following extract from the last one he wrote to me is given as an interesting souvenir of a brave and upright man'

Translation of letter (reproduced on page 93)

Finally, sir, I very much regret that I have committed myself with your countryman and am unable to accompany you in your conquests, but once one has given one's word, one must keep it and be a man

So have patience for the duration of this campaign, and let us hope that we shall meet again later

Meanwhile, please accept the humble salutations of your utterly devoted

Croz Michel-Auguste

On June 29th, led by Christian Almer, who became his chief guide, and by Franz Biener, Whymper achieved the first ascent of the Aiguille Verte by the couloir that has since borne his name

On July 3rd the same team made the first crossing of the Col de Talèfre and reached Courmayeur. Whymper writes with satisfaction: 'All of the excursions that were set down in my programme had been carried out with the exception of the ascent of the Matterhorn . . . .'

On the 7th he crossed the Valcournera pass to get to Breuil. 'My thoughts were fixed on the Matterhorn.

right-hand page
The east face of the Matterhorn. Photo: Gaston Rébuffat
pages 90-91
The Matterhorn seen from the Riffelhorn
Photo: Gaston Rébuffat

and my guides knew that I wished them to accompany me. They had an aversion to the mountain, and repeatedly expressed their belief that it was useless to try to ascend it. "*Anything* but Matterhorn, dear Sir!" said Almer; "*anything* but Matterhorn." He did not speak of difficulty or of danger, nor was he shirking *work*. He offered to go *anywhere*; but he entreated that the Matterhorn should be abondoned.

Once more the young Englishman was facing his only real objective alone and defenceless. From now on, however, events were to develop at a crazy speed: the ascent of the Matterhorn, which could on many occasions have been achieved in an atmosphere of calm and good humour, was to be prepared, decided and carried out in an atmosphere of frenzy, secretiveness, almost of conspiracy – and of extreme emotionalism. In the midst of the continuous 'general post', tempers became frayed and were exacerbated as never before.

On the evening of July 7th Whymper arrived at Valtournanche. He went off at once in search of Jean-Antoine Carrel. He was not there. The villagers told Whymper that the 'Bersagliere' had set out on the 6th with three companions to attempt the climb on their own account. Whymper was cheered by the fact that

above
Part of the letter Michel Croz wrote to Whymper explaining that he was unable to accompany him on his expedition

left-hand page
The Matterhorn seen from Breuil
Photo: Alfonso Bernardi

pages 94-95
Profile of the Hörnli arête, at the height of the 'Shoulder'
Photo: Bradford Washburn

DICHET

the weather was bad. He went straight away up to Breuil, thinking to meet them. Halfway there, he observed a group on the other side of the valley. He hurried towards them, and, as expected, found Jean-Antoine and César Carrel, C.-E. Gorret and J.-J. Maquignaz. The bad weather had prevented them from going any further.

Whymper, from then onwards quite determined on the Hörnli arête, explained his intentions to Carrel, and asked him to accompany him. Jean-Antoine would have preferred to return to the Italian ridge, but finally agreed. Whymper parted company with Almer and Biener, who were absolutely opposed to the idea of going up the Matterhorn.

On the 8th storms threatened, and the day was taken up with preparations.

On the 9th, on descending to Valtournanche, Whymper met 'a foreign tourist' followed by a mule and several porters loaded with baggage, and among them Jean-Antoine and César carrying barometers. Whymper, surprised, asked for an explanation. The foreigner, they said, had arrived just when they were setting out, and they had given his porters a helping hand.

'Very well,' Whymper answered, 'go to Breuil. We will leave at midnight as agreed.'

'But I can only accompany you until Tuesday, the 11th, because I have an engagement with a family of distinction.'

'And César?'

'César too.'

'Why did you not tell me this sooner?'

'Because it had not been decided. I was retained a long time ago,' Carrel went on, 'but the day was not fixed. On Friday evening, when I got back to Valtournanche after leaving you, I found a letter telling me the day I had to hold myself in readiness.'

All this was strictly accurate; moreover, Whymper concluded: 'I could not object to the answer; still the prospect of being guideless was provoking.'

The east face of the Matterhorn; on the extreme left, the Lion arête; on the left, further forward, the Furggen arête, on the right, the Hörnli arête.
Drawing by Pierre Bichet

At the end of the day the weather was frightful; it was pouring with rain. Whymper came upon Carrel by chance under the church porch.

'I thought you were in Breuil,' the Englishman said to Jean-Antoine.

'When the storm burst, it was clear that we could not set out this evening, and so I came down to sleep here.'

'This is a great bore,' Whymper retorted. 'If tomorrow is not fine, we shall not be able to do anything together. Relying on you, I have sent away my guides, and you leave me for a party of ladies. That work is not fit for *you*; can't you send someone else instead?'

'No, monsieur, I am very sorry, but my word is pledged. I should like to accompany you, but I cannot break my engagement.'

'Well, it is no fault of yours,' Whymper said. 'Come presently with César and have some wine.' This settled nothing. They plunged a little deeper into misunderstanding.

It is true that Whymper, counting on Carrel, had parted company with Almer and Biener. But, Whymper has made it quite clear that the two Swiss guides, despite their excellent qualities, were unwilling in any circumstances to go up the Matterhorn, so the young Englishman had lost nothing so far as they were concerned. He had engaged Carrel, but the usually precise Whymper does not indicate anywhere until what date. Jean-Antoine could not have accepted a long engagement, and had not made the slightest promise. Furthermore, the weather was bad. Whatever the rights and wrongs of the matter, Carrel, a proud man, was uncomfortable about the misunderstanding. He did not lie, but he avoided speaking clearly. As long as only he and Whymper were involved, it was a simple matter, but Carrel was no longer a lone wolf. Everything had become more complex.

On the 10th it rained again throughout the day. In Breuil Whymper said goodbye to Jean-Antoine and César.

On the 11th a friend came to wake Whymper to ask him if he had heard the news. 'No, what news?' 'What!' the other said. 'Don't you know? A large party of guides set off this morning to try to climb the Matterhorn.'

Whymper could see the advancing party clearly with a telescope. Favre, the innkeeper, was present.

'What does all this mean?' Whymper demanded.

'Who is the leader of these guides?' 'Carrel,' Favre replied. 'What! Jean-Antoine?' 'Yes, Jean-Antoine.' 'And is César with him?' 'Certainly.'

'Then I saw in a moment that I had been bamboozled and humbugged,' Whymper writes bitterly, 'and learned, bit by bit, that the affair had been arranged long beforehand. The start on the 6th had been for a preliminary reconnaissance; the mule, that I passed, was conveying stores for the attack; the "family of distinction" was Signor F. Giordano, who had just despatched the party to facilitate the way to the summit, and who, when the facilitation was completed, was to be taken to the top along with Signor Sella!"

Whymper had not been tricked, and no one had made a fool of him. The truth is that, despite the evidence, Whymper, for all his extreme clear-headedness and efficiency, had never understood or wanted to understand, and even less to admit, that Carrel would not go to the summit with him. It was not that Jean-Antoine did not respect him, or even admire him, but simply that that was how matters stood; and at this point in the story it is fair to recall that Carrel had not once made the slightest promise or even given the slightest encouragement that might have led Whymper to believe collaboration between them at all possible. Very much to the contrary! For years the Englishman had clung to the idea, the hope of going with Carrel, as one clings to an illusion. It is true that there was no other guide there who was tempted by the adventure, but that is not an adequate reason for Whymper's having deluded himself until the last moment, or at least for his having forced himself to deny the evidence.

Carrel had changed slightly in the last year. He had been more at ease, even in his unsociable moments, when he had been working alone. In this month of July 1865, Jean-Antoine was no longer completely himself and himself alone; the fine and noble natural pride of the 'Bersagliere' sorted ill with certain misunderstandings. He was doubtless gratified and honoured to be invited to take part in a 'great enterprise', but at times, perhaps, he regretted the much-cherished total independence he had to a small extent surrendered.

Here is the account of the situation that Guido Rey gives in his book on the Matterhorn: 'In his preface to the first volume of the *Alpine Journal* of London, published in 1863, the editor, Mr H. B. George, after

Lord Francis Douglas. From the collection of Emile Gos.
Peter Taugwalder, jun. Drawing by Edward Whymper,
photo: Hachette

pages 100-101 Tête du Cervin, east side. Photo: Peters

making it known that nearly all the highest Alpine
peaks had now been conquered, wrote these words,
which sounded like a trumpet-call to English climbers:
"When all the other attractions of the Swiss Alps have
been exhausted for us, there still remains, and will
remain no one knows how long yet, the Matterhorn,
unconquered and apparently unconquerable".'

In Switzerland no one had any desire to attack the
celebrated peak, Swiss though it was on three of its faces.
In Italy, on the other hand, this passage had aroused
bitter feeling. In July 1863, in Turin, a small group of
intelligent and energetic young men held a meeting at
the Château Valentine to plan the creation of an Italian
Alpine Club: Quintino Sella, Bartolomeo Gastaldi and
Felix Giordano were the originators of the idea and the
leaders in taking action. 'There, in secret,' Guido Rey
continues, 'the question was mooted of making the
great venture so that some of its glory would be reflected
upon the institution at its birth. English climbers had
snatched from the Italians the first conquest of Monte
Viso, the supreme Peak of Piedmont; there remained
the Matterhorn: it was marked out as the victim.

'They were aware of the clandestine attempts made
by the Valtournanche guides; the ground seemed to
have been promisingly prepared. Neither Gastaldi, for
reasons of character, nor Sella, because of heavy com-
mitments, could have taken the responsibility of study-
ing and preparing the enterprise: the exacting honour
was offered to Giordano, who accepted it.'

Meanwhile Sella entrusted one of his friends, Giuseppe
Torelli, a politician and an elegant writer, with the
mission of seeking out Jean-Antoine and sending him
to Sella at his home in Biella. Torelli found Carrel and
admired him, and after half an hour's conversation
persuaded him to yield to his request and go for the
interview that Sella wanted.

During the summer of 1864, Carrel met Giordano at
the Théodule Pass. Then they spent a whole evening
together at Giomein, above Breuil, in the company of
Canon Carrel.

A few days later Giordano was at Sella's home in
Biella.

The winter passed, plans took shape, and Whymper
suspected nothing. It was only on July 11th that he
realized that the 'family of distinction' was none other
than the engineer Giordano.

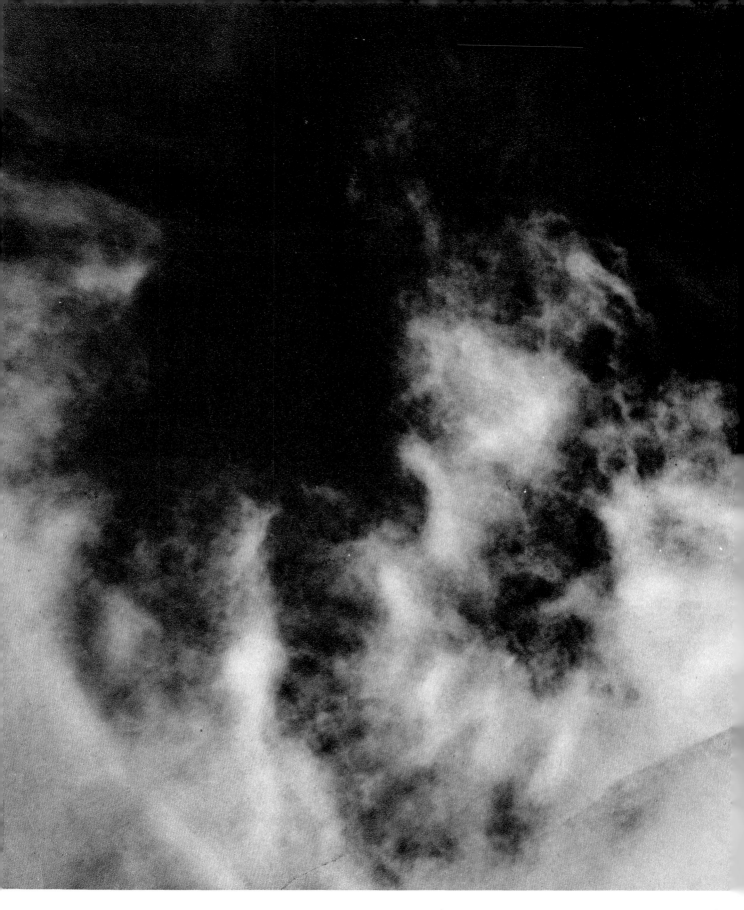

On the evening of that same day Giordano wrote to Sella to keep him abreast of the news.

'The Breuil Inn, at the foot of the Théodule, the evening of July 11th.

'It is time I gave you some news from here. I was at Valtournanche at noon on Saturday the 8th. I met Carrel there. He was returning from an attempted reconnaissance on the Matterhorn, which had failed because of bad weather. Whymper had arrived two or three days earlier. As usual, he wanted to make an ascent, and had engaged Carrel, who, not having yet received my letters, had agreed, on condition, however, that the engagement should be for a few days only. Luckily the weather got worse. Whymper could not undertake his new attempt, and Carrel, being free once more, joined me, bringing me five other picked men who are the best guides in the valley. The preparatory expedition, with Carrel as leader, was organized immediately: so as not to attract attention we carried the ropes and other material to a fairly remote chalet below the Matterhorn (Avouil). And this chalet will be our advance headquarters.

'Of the six men, four will work up above, and two will act continuously as porters, a job which is at least as difficult. As for me, I intend to stay in Breuil for the moment.

'The weather, our terrible deity on whom everything will depend, has up to now been extremely changeable and rather bad. Yesterday morning it was snowing on the Matterhorn, but yesterday evening it seemed to clear up.

'During the night (10-11), the men set off with the tents, and I hope that by now they are fairly high; however, mist is spreading again, and the Mattérhorn is completely covered; I hope they are only passing mists. Weather permitting, I think that in three or four days I shall have a good idea of what the prospects are likely to be.

'Carrel has advised me on no account to go up until he sends me word. Naturally, he insists on verifying the final details personally. Looking at the rocks from here, they do not seem to be absolutely inaccessible, but I realize that before one can judge that, one must know them better. And it is necessary, too, to see if it will be possible to set up a bivouac in a much higher place than the one where Whymper established his.

From top to bottom
The Reverend Charles Hudson. From the collection of Emile Gos
Peter Taugwalder, sen. From the collection of Emile Gos
D. Robert Hadow. From the collection of Emile Gos

102

As soon as I have favourable news, I will send an express messenger to Saint-Vincent, which is the nearest telegraph office, with a telegram in a few words. And then you will come immediately . . . . .

'Meanwhile, as soon as you receive my letter, do me the favour of writing me a couple of lines in reply, so that I may know, one way or another, what to expect, because here I am beset by difficulties, namely, the weather, the expense, and Whymper. I have done my best to keep all this secret; but that man, whose life seems to depend on the Matterhorn, is here, full of suspicions, and spying on every moment.

'I have taken all the capable men away from him, but so passionate is he about this mountain that he could climb with others and still bring off some dramatic coup. He is here in the same inn as I am, but I carefully avoid talking to him. In short, I will do all I can to make this affair a success—and I hope that the winds will favour us! . . . .

'I shall write nothing more, in the expectation of soon being able to send you the good news. I hope *this* news, coming from the Alps, will afford you some little relief from the hot oppressiveness of Turin and the Ministry.'

Everything was clear. 'My plans were upset,' Whymper writes. 'The Italians had clearly stolen a march upon me. What was to be done?' Whymper calmed his nerves by smoking a cigar and thinking. Hope was soon kindled as he counted the points in his favour. 'They have taken a mule's load of provisions. That is *one* point in my favour, for they will take two or three days to get through the food, and, until that is done, no work will be accomplished.' "How is the weather?" I went to the window. The mountain was smothered up in mist. "Another point in my favour." "They are to facilitate the way. Well, if they do that to any purpose, it will be a long job".'

Whymper felt calmer. Leaving no eventuality out of his account, he adds: 'It was evident that the wily ones might be outwitted after all. There was time enough to go to Zermatt, to try the eastern face, and, should it prove impracticable, to come back to Breuil before the men returned; and then, it seemed to me, as the mountain was not padlocked, one might start at the same time as the Messieurs, and yet get to the top before them.'

But he had still to be able to get to Zermatt. Now, all the guides and porters had been taken; even the little hunchback, Luc Maynet, could not come: it was the most important season for his cheese-making.

'I was in the position of a general without an army; it was all very well to make plans, but there was no one to execute them. This did not much trouble me, for it was evident that so long as the weather stopped traffic over the Théodule, it would hinder the men equally upon the Matterhorn; and I knew that directly it improved company would certainly arrive.' And Whymper hoped, or rather, expected, to join them when they returned to Zermatt.

Towards noon a fairly large party of tourists arrived in Breuil. 'A nimble young Englishman' walked ahead, accompanied by one of old Peter Taugwalder's sons. Whymper ran to the young Englishman to ask him if he could let him have Taugwalder. That was not possible, for both of them were due to return to Zermatt the following morning. However, the young guide, having nothing to carry, could very well take Whymper's baggage.

So all was not lost. During the afternoon Whymper recounted his disappointments to the young Englishman, who was Lord Francis Douglas; he, aged only eighteen, had just accomplished a fine first ascent: that of the north face of the Ober Gabelhorn. From that peak, and during the whole descent, he had been able to admire the Matterhorn, and above all to establish that the Hörnli arête, which, when viewed from Zermatt directly opposite, appeared so steep, had a very acceptable slope when seen from the truest angle, namely, in profile. Moreover, old Peter Taugwalder had climbed beyond the Hörnli a few days before, and had declared that the ascent seemed feasible to him.

The young lord more or less secretly dreamed of climbing the Matterhorn. He had come to Breuil to contact Carrel, and fate had willed that he should come across Whymper; without more ado, agreement was reached. The plans that had been slowly and carefully worked out were irrevocably abandoned in order to plunge into a succession of improvisations.

The next morning Whymper, Douglas and young Peter, assisted by a porter finally lent by Favre, the innkeeper, crossed the Col du Théodule, heavily laden but with hearts full of hope. During the descent they deposited the tents, blankets and ropes in the little chapel at the Schwarzsee.

Upon arriving in Zermatt, Whymper and Douglas engaged old Peter and authorized him to choose another guide; so everything was arranged. And yet, immediately, there was to be a return to complete uncertainty: the first person Whymper met on returning to the Monte Rosa Hotel was none other than Michel Croz. What was he doing there?

His English client, Mr B., had arrived at Chamonix ill, and immediately returned to London. Croz, released from his engagement, had been hired straight away by the Reverend Charles Hudson, and the two had just arrived in Zermatt with the intention of climbing the Matterhorn!

Whymper and Douglas were finishing dinner at the 'Monte Rosa' when the clergyman came into the dining-room with a friend. They had just inspected the Matterhorn, and Hudson confirmed to some tourists that they would set off early the following morning to attempt the climb.

For years Whymper had been alone; now Matterhorn climbers were fairly jostling one another.

Whymper and Douglas went out to confer together: 'We agreed it was undesirable that two independent parties should be on the mountain at the same time with the same object.' So they went to invite the Reverend Hudson to join forces with them.

It was difficult, doubtless impossible, to do otherwise. Yet Whymper, aware of the inconvenience of attempting the climb in such numbers, must have hesitated an uncommonly long time; but finally, by accepting Hudson, he won back Croz; that was the important factor.

Hudson accepted the proposition, but on one condition – that his friend Mr Hadow should take part in the expedition. Once again everything was back in the melting-pot. Whymper hesitated, and enquired about the climbs the young man had done.

'Mr Hadow has done Mont Blanc in less time than most men.'

It is surprising that such a frivolous, stupid and above all muddle-headed reply should have come from Hudson; the ascent of Mont Blanc, a snow mountain, has nothing in common with the rock-climb of the Matterhorn.

Hudson mentioned, in addition, several other excursions to Hadow's credit 'that were unknown to me,' Whymper points out and the clergyman concluded by saying: 'I consider he is a sufficiently good man to go with us.'

Whymper adds: 'Mr Hadow was admitted without any further question, and we then went into the matter of guides. Hudson thought that Croz and old Peter would be sufficient. The question was referred to the men themselves, and they made no objection.'

'So Croz and I became comrades once more,' writes Whymper. In these words of hope there was great tenderness and the promise of good luck! 'As I threw myself on my bed and tried to go to sleep, I wondered at the strange series of chances which had first separated us and then brought us together again. I thought of the mistake through which he had accepted the engagement to Mr B.; of his unwillingness to adopt my route; of his recommendation to transfer our energies to the chain of Mont Blanc; of the retirement of Almer and Biener; of the desertion of Carrel; of the arrival of Lord Francis Douglas; and, lastly, of our accidental meeting at Zermatt; and as I pondered over these things I could not help asking, "What next?" If any one of the links of this fatal chain of circumstances had been omitted, what a different story I should have to tell!'

The east face of the Matterhorn. Photo: Pierre Bichet

THE CONQUEST

'We started from Zermatt on the 13th July 1865, at half-past five, on a brilliant and perfectly cloudless morning,' writes Whymper. 'We were eight in number: Croz, old Peter Taugwalder and his two sons, taken as porters (the following morning one was to take part in the ascent, the other would return to Zermatt), Lord Francis Douglas, Hadow, Hudson and I.'

It was a strange party, heavily laden and ill assorted, that set out, not on a basis of unhurried and carefully thought out preparation and agreement, but because of a trick of fate and the force of circumstances.

To attempt the first ascent of the 'most inaccessible peak', men were to find themselves roped together without knowing one another, and almost in spite of themselves. It is clear that Whymper had joined forces with Douglas (whom he had not known forty-eight hours earlier) only because, being alone, he had had no other

left-hand page
The Matterhorn seen from the chalets of Zermatt.
Photo: Pierre Tairraz

pages 108-109
The Matterhorn: on the left, the east face; facing, the Hörnli arête; on the right, the north face.
Photo: Bradford Washburn

pages 110-111
The summit of the Matterhorn from the north-east, with the Hörnli shoulder in the foreground.
Photo: Bradford Washburn

course open to him, short of giving up. To give up was unthinkable for Whymper, and, above all, would have been unfair. He and Douglas on the one hand, and Hudson on the other, had come to a fresh agreement only to avoid the presence of two independent teams on the mountain at the same time! Finally, Whymper had accepted the company of Hadow, insisted upon by Hudson, only because by doing so, he would get Croz back – a curious piece of bargaining! Could he have done otherwise? With such a series of uncertainties and improvisations it was a question of take it or leave it.

A strange rendezvous fixed by destiny! Each of them had boarded a moving train, and Whymper had come within a hair's breadth of missing it! As to the spirit of the venture, it was a long caravan of individual ambitions, tied to the same rope, which climbed towards the Matterhorn. It is true that their departure had been an urgent one, for each of them was thinking of the Italians who were already on the other ridge; and each would give of his best.

They all wished for victory, but one of them more than the others. Douglas, Hadow, Hudson . . . it was the first time they had set out for the mountain; for Whymper it was the ninth. For five years he had dreamed of nothing but this decisive moment, and today, pressed by Carrel to bring matters to a head, he would have roped himself with the devil. At least Michel Croz was there, and after the delays and disappointments, and in the midst of the countless concessions Whymper had had to accept concerning himself and others, the presence of the companion

of great moments and difficult times seemed to him like a ray of hope and a guarantee of security.

Michel Croz had agreed to guide this heterogeneous caravan. Had he really had the choice? Had he been influenced? Was it the lure of gain, the desire for victory, or was it generosity–reluctance to turn down Hudson, who had hired him, and Whymper, whom he respected and for whom a refusal would have been a serious affront . . . and reluctance to disappoint Whymper?

How could Hudson, a confirmed alpinist, who had achieved great first ascents, and in particular the Aiguille Verte, by way of the Arête du Moine, with Michel Croz only eight days before; who had, as much as ten years earlier, climbed Mont Blanc by way of the Aiguille du Goûter, for the first time and without a guide–how could he have pushed forward Hadow, a young man of eighteen, for such an ascent, and forced him on the party, when his only experience was the ascent of Mont Blanc, in a fairly fast time it is true, but without 'knowing how to belay', as T. S. Kennedy, who was with him, was to point out. Mont Blanc furthermore was only a snow ascent, requiring stamina, certainly, but needing no special technique, and in any case, no rock-climbing skill.

Anyhow, the strange caravan climbed towards the Schwarzsee, recovered the equipment left the previous day by Whymper, stopped there for a while, continued on its way, stopped again to study the route, resumed the climbing and then set up camp.

Croz and the young Taugwalder pushed on up to reconnoitre, and came back with good news: they had met with no difficulty.

Hudson made tea, Whymper coffee, then they all wrapped themselves in their sleeping bags. Douglas and Whymper occupied the tent with the Taugwalders, while the others bivouacked in the open.

Before falling asleep, they had naturally thought of the Italians. But they were not really worried. That night, on the Hörnli arête, hope was in every heart.

On the 14th, the whole team was up before dawn, and started climbing as soon as it was light enough for them to find their way, following at first the itinerary reconnoitred the previous day by Croz and the young Taugwalder. Except in a few places the climbers were not roped together. Hudson and Whymper took turns to lead; for the time being the climbing was not difficult.

They made their first halt at 12,675 feet, at 6.20 a.m., and a second halt at the Shoulder 'at 9.55' as Whymper noted precisely .

'We had now arrived at the foot of that part which, from the Riffelberg or from Zermatt, seems perpendicular or overhanging.' The easy part had come to an end; now success was in the balance.

A change in the order of the rope had become necessary. 'Croz went first, I followed,' pointed out Whymper, 'Hudson came third; Hadow and old Peter were last. "Now," said Croz, as he led off, "now for something altogether different." The work became difficult and required caution. In some places there was little to hold, and it was desirable that those should be in front who were least likely to slip.' The slope was not very steep, but owing to the bad weather of the preceeding days, conditions were not good. 'The snow,' Whymper went on, 'had accumulated in, and had filled up, the interstices of the rock-face, leaving only occasional fragments projecting here and there. These were at times covered with a thin film of ice, produced from the melting and refreezing of the snow,'

Apart from Croz, who was leading, Hudson was the one who was the most at his ease: 'He required not the slightest assistance,' points out Whymper, who adds: 'Sometimes, after I had taken a hand from Croz, or received a pull, I turned to offer the same to Hudson; but he invariably declined, saying it was not necessary. Mr Hadow, however, was not accustomed to this kind of work, and required continual assistance. It is only fair to say that the difficulty which he found at this part arose simply and entirely from want of experience.'

Fortunately, 'this solitary difficult part was of no great extent.' After a long traverse on the north face, then the scaling of a projection of about sixty feet, Croz could rejoin the arête, and climb the red rocks. 'A long stride round a rather awkward corner,' and they reached the snow of the last slopes.

'The last doubt vanished! The Matterhorn was ours! Nothing but 200 feet of easy snow remained to be surmounted!'

Now that there was no further doubt about reaching the summit, Whymper thought immediately of Carrel. Which of the two, he or the 'Bersagliere' was going to be the victor in this pitiless race?

'You must now carry your thoughts back to the seven

Italians who started from Breuil on the 11th July,' wrote Whymper. 'Four days had passed since their departure, and we were tormented with anxiety lest they should arrive on the top before us. All the way up we had talked of them, and many false alarms of "men on the summit" had been raised. The higher we rose, the more intense became the excitement. What if we should be beaten at the last moment?'

Whymper could stand it no longer; the last members of the team, still in the difficult passages, were slowing down the advance of the first who had just reached the last phase of the ascent, of moderate gradient and easy. 'The slope eased off,' says Whymper, 'at length we could be detached, and Croz and I, dashing away, ran a neck-and-neck race, which ended in a dead heat. At 1.40 p.m. the world was at our feet, and the Matterhorn was conquered. Hurrah! Not a footstep could be seen.

'It was not yet certain that we had not been beaten.'

The Matterhorn has two summits – the Swiss summit to the north and the Italian summit to the south, joined by a ridge about 350 feet long. Whymper was seized with doubt. They were at the north summit, had the Italians already reached the south summit?

'I hastened to the southern end, scanning the snow right and left eagerly. Hurrah! again; it was untrodden.'

Whymper was jubilant and almost surprised not to find Carrel either on the summit or at least not far from it.

'Where were the men? I peered over the cliff, half doubting, half expectant, and saw them immediately – mere dots on the ridge, at an immense distance below. Up went my arms and my hat. "Croz! Croz! come here!" "Where are they, Monsieur?" "There, don't you see them, down there?" "Ah! the *coquins*, they are low down." "Croz, we must make those fellows hear us." We yelled until we were hoarse. The Italians seemed to regard us – we could not be certain. "Croz, we *must* make them hear us; they *shall* hear us!" I seized a block of rock and hurled it down, and called upon my companion, in the name of friendship, to do the same. We drove our sticks in, and prized away the crags, and soon a torrent of stones poured down the cliffs. There was no mistake about it this time. The Italians turned and fled.'

After these mad and noisy victory demonstrations, Whymper seems to have experienced feelings of remorse or at least of regret. True, he could be generous, since he had won, yet there was no doubt that Whymper, deep down, had wished that Carrel, whose courage he admired, and who in many ways resembled him, could have been by his side on this great day.

'I would that the leader of that party could have stood with us at that moment, for our victorious shouts conveyed to him the disappointment of the ambition of a lifetime. He was *the* man, of all those who attempted the ascent of the Matterhorn, who most deserved to be the first upon its summit. He was the first to doubt its inaccessibility, and he was the only man who persisted in believing that its ascent would be accomplished. It was the aim of his life to make the ascent from the side of Italy, for the honour of his native valley. For a time he had the game in his hands: he played it as he thought best: but he made a false move, and he lost it.'

Now, Whymper, Croz and the other members of the victorious team returned, reassured, towards the north summit. 'Croz now took the tent-pole, and planted it in the highest snow. "Yes," we said, "there is the flag-staff, but where is the flag?" "Here it is," he answered, pulling off his blouse and fixing it to the stick. It made a poor flag, and there was no wind to float it out, yet it was seen all around. They saw it at Zermatt – at the Riffel – in the Val Tournanche.'

In fact, from Breuil too, men had been seen on the summit of the Matterhorn; Giordano at once wrote to Sella to tell him – cruel error – that Carrel had been victorious.

'Inn of Breuil, 14th July.

'Dear Quintino, I am sending by express messenger a cable addressed to you to Saint-Vincent, which is about seven hours' walk from here. At the same time, to make doubly sure, I am posting this letter to your address.

'At two o'clock this afternoon, I could, with a good telescope, make out Carrel and the others on the very top of the Matterhorn; others with me have seen them. Our success therefore seems certain, and this despite the fact that the weather was very bad the day before yesterday, and the mountain was completely covered with snow.

pages 114-115
'Ascent of the Matterhorn, July 14th, 1865; arrival at the summit'. Drawing by Whymper

113

'So leave immediately if you can; if you cannot, send me a telegram to Saint-Vincent. I do not even know if you are in Turin! For a week I have had no news from there; I am therefore just taking a chance with this letter. If you do not come or send a telegram by tomorrow, I shall go to be the first to plant our flag up there. It is a necessary gesture. However, I shall do my best to wait for you so that you can come yourself. Whymper set off to attempt the ascent from the other side, but, I think, in vain.'

At Breuil, the enthusiasm was great; disillusionment was to be all the more painful.

Above, Whymper and his companions returned to the Italian summit to put up a cairn, a sign of their having been there, proof of their victory. The absolutely clear weather and the profound stillness somewhat calmed the agitation of these great and at the same time weak men. They admired the fabulous view, which as far as they could see and wherever they turned, was theirs. The purity of the atmosphere that day ensured exceptional visibility over all the summits of the Alps.

'I see them clearly now,' notes Whymper in his account, '–the great inner circles of giants, backed by the ranges, chains, and massifs. First came the Dent Blanche, hoary and grand; the Gabelhorn and pointed Rothorn; and then the peerless Weisshorn; the towering Mischabelhörner, flanked by the Allalinhorn, Stahlhorn, and Rimpfischhorn; then Monte Rosa—with its many Spitzes–the Lyskamm and the Breithorn. Behind were the Bernese Oberland, governed by the Finsteraarhorn; the Simplon and St Gotthard groups; the Disgrazia and the Ortler. Towards the south we looked down to Chivasso on the plain of Piedmont, and far beyond. The Viso—one hundred miles away–seemed close upon us; the Maritime Alps—one hundred and thirty miles distant –were free from haze. Then came my first love–the Pelvoux, the Écrins and the Meije; the clusters of the Graians; and lastly, in the west, glowing in full sunlight, rose the monarch of all—Mont Blanc.'

Everywhere the light was soft, magnificent, peaceful. Now, their gaze dropped to the fields of Zermatt. the pastures of Breuil.

'There were forests black and gloomy, and meadows bright and lively; bounding waterfalls and tranquil lakes; fertile lands and savage wastes; sunny plains and frigid plateaux. There were the most rugged forms, and the most graceful outlines–bold, perpendicular cliffs, and gentle undulating slopes; rocky mountains and snowy mountains, sombre and solemn, or glittering and white, with walls–turrets–pinnacles–pyramids– domes–cones–and spires! There was every combination that the world can give, and every contrast that the heart could desire.

'We remained on the summit for one hour–
"One crowded hour of glorious life."
It passed away too quickly, and we began to prepare for the descent.'

THE DESCENT

'Hudson and I again consulted as to the best and safest arrangement of the party. We agreed that it would be best for Croz to go first, and Hadow second; Hudson, who was almost equal to a born mountaineer in sureness of foot, wished to be third; Lord Francis Douglas was placed next, and old Peter, the strongest of the remainder, after him.'

After the ebullience of victory, and the serene pleasure of contemplation, did they realize, Whymper, Hudson and their companions, that their greatest difficulties still lay before them?

The ascent had been achieved more easily than Whymper had expected, but one part was, in his own words 'really difficult': this was where they had gone over on to the north face, about 260 feet below the summit, at the place where Hadow 'owing to his lack of experience', had been uneasy, and where they had met some snow on the rocks that morning which that afternoon could very well have turned to verglas.

During the descent, nervous tension was greater, the holds were hard to find, the drop was more alarming.

Whymper, always clear-minded, except on one point which was to prove fatal, suggested to Hudson the use of fixed ropes when they reached the difficult part: the reverend gentleman approved this idea, but it was not definitely settled that it should be done.'

right-hand page
From the summit of the Matterhorn, looking down on the north glacier of the Matterhorn. Photo: Gaston Rébuffat
pages 118-119
The shadow of the Matterhorn. Photo: Gaston Rébuffat

It was nearly three o'clock; it was already late; Whymper finished a sketch and was about to rope himself in the middle of the team, 'when someone remembered that our names had not been left in a bottle. They requested me to write them down, and moved off while it was being done'.

Whymper must have tasted a supreme moment of happiness, alone on the summit of the Matterhorn. Then the great mountain was once restored to silence and solitude. Whymper roped himself with the young Taugwalder, who had been waiting for him, and 'running after' their companions, they rejoined them at the moment when they were just 'commencing the descent of the difficult part'.

'For some little distance we two followed the others, detached from them, and should have continued so had not Lord Francis Douglas asked me, about 3 p.m., to tie on to old Peter, as he feared, he said, that Taugwalder would not be able to hold his ground if a slip occurred.'

It was done, the terrible word had been spoken: a slip! Uncertainty gripped the team.

Yet the most elaborate precautions had been taken: 'Only one man was moving at a time; when he was firmly planted the next advanced, and so on. They had not, however, attached the additional rope to rocks, and nothing was said about it. The suggestion was not made for my own sake, and I am not sure that it even occurred to me again.'

In short, the seven men were now roped all together: Croz, right at the bottom, led the way down; Hadow followed him, then came Hudson, Douglas, Taugwalder, sen., Whymper and Taugwalder, jun. It is possible that the fact that there were seven of them and that they were all roped together gave them an illusion of sureness and strength; yet Douglas, who was right in the middle and able to see everything, was uneasy; at that moment, no doubt, he was the most clear-minded.

Hudson, on the other hand, was sure of himself,

and he was right; but was he sure of the others, and in particular of Hadow, who was below him, and for whose safety he was responsible?

'A few minutes later,' wrote Whymper, 'a sharp-eyed lad ran into the Monte Rosa Hotel, to Seiler, saying that he had seen an avalanche fall from the summit of the Matterhorn on to the Matterhorn Glacier. The boy was reproved for telling idle stories; he was right, nevertheless, and this was what he saw.

'Michel Croz had laid aside his axe, and in order to give Mr Hadow greater security, was absolutely taking hold of his legs, and putting his feet, one by one, into their proper positions. So far as I know, no one was actually descending. I cannot speak with certainty, because the two leading men were partially hidden from my sight by an intervening mass of rock, but it is my belief, from the movements of their shoulders, that Croz, having done as I have said, was in the act of turning round, to go down a step or two himself; at this moment Mr Hadow slipped, fell against him, and knocked him over. I heard one startled exclamation from Croz, then saw him and Mr Hadow flying downwards; in another moment Hudson was dragged from his steps, and Lord Francis Douglas immediately after him. All this was the work of a moment.'

With all their strength, Whymper and Taugwalder, sen., clung to the rocks; almost at once, as powerful as it was sudden, came the jerk of the sudden tautening of the rope between the four slipping bodies and Taugwalder, sen.

'We held; but the rope broke midway between Taugwalder and Lord Francis Douglas. For a few seconds we saw our unfortunate companions sliding downwards on their backs, and spreading out their hands, endeavouring to save themselves. They passed from our sight uninjured, disappeared one by one, and fell from precipice to precipice onto the Matterhorn Glacier below, a distance of nearly 4,000 feet in height. From the moment the rope broke it was impossible to help them.

'So perished our comrades!'

A few days later, during his first interrogation by the Valais government, Taugwalder, sen., was to describe the accident in a slightly different way: 'It was there that the first tourist (Hadow) slipped and dragged with him those who followed him (Hudson and Douglas), and these dragged with them the guide

left-hand page
The Italian arête from Tyndall Peak. Photo: Pierre Tairraz

pages 122-123
'The ascent of the Matterhorn, July 14th, 1865; the fall.
Lithograph from a drawing by Gustave Doré (detail)

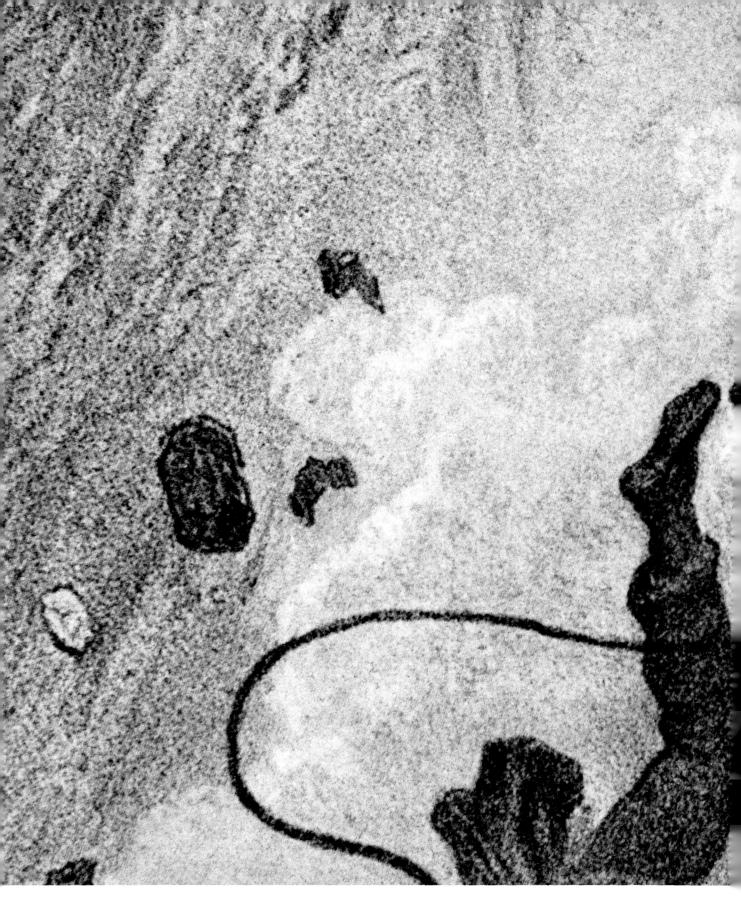

Croz, after the rope between Lord Douglas and me had broken.' However, during his second interrogation, after the judge had pointed out to him the difference between his statement and that of Whymper, he was to say: 'As Mr Whymper was above me in a position from which he could observe this unfortunate accident, it could be that his statement was much more accurate, so I do not want to maintain any longer that Croz fell after the other three tourists.'

Whymper, who was to be marked for ever by that accident, pointed out again in a note in his book: 'Mr Hadow slipped off his feet on to his back, his feet struck Croz in the small of the back, and knocked him right over, head first. Croz's axe was out of his reach, and without it he managed to get his head uppermost before he disappeared from our sight. If it had been in his hand I have no doubt that he would have stopped himself and Mr Hadow.'

It is true that Croz was very strong, but on a rock wall, it is very improbable that his ice axe could have helped him to check a fall. 'Mr Hadow, at the moment of the slip,' Whymper went on, 'was not occupying a bad position. He could have moved either up or down, and could touch with his hand the rock of which I have spoken. Hudson was not so well placed, but he had liberty of motion. The rope was not taut from him to Hadow, and the two men fell ten or twelve feet before the jerk upon him. Lord F. Douglas was not favourably placed, and could neither move up nor down. Old Peter was firmly planted, and stood just beneath a large rock which he hugged with both arms. I enter into these details to make it more apparent that the position occupied by the party at the moment of the accident was not by any means excessively trying. We were compelled to pass over the exact spot where the slip occurred, and we found – even with shaken nerves – that it was not a difficult place to pass. I have described the *slope generally* as difficult, and it is so undoubtedly to most persons; but it must be distinctly understood that Mr Hadow slipped at a comparatively easy part.'

Taugwalder, sen., to whom the tribunal was to ask the following question, (Q. 31): 'Do you think that all possible precautions had been taken at that spot?' was to answer: 'Yes. It is, however, regrettable that the first person after Croz (Hadow) should have been

a very bad climber,' and, one may add, equipped with boots which were in very bad condition.

Stunned by what they had just seen, the three survivors were petrified. 'For the space of half an hour,' wrote Whymper, 'we remained on the spot without moving a single step. The two men, paralysed by terror, cried like infants, and trembled in such a manner as to threaten us with the fate of the others. Old Peter rent the air with exclamations of "Chamonix! Oh, what will Chamonix say?" He meant, who would believe that Croz could fall? The young man did nothing but scream or sob, "We are lost! we are lost!" Fixed between the two I could neither move up nor down.'

Whymper begged young Peter to descend, but he was terrified and did not dare to take one step. Old Peter became alive to the danger and started to shout: 'We are lost! Lost!'

Finally, after these minutes of extreme tension, young Peter decided to move down and the three men stood together again.

'Immediately,' writes Whymper, 'I asked for the rope which had given way, and found, to my surprise – indeed to my horror – that it was the weakest of the three ropes. It was not brought, and should not have been employed, for the purpose for which it was used. It was old rope, and, compared with the others, was feeble. It was intended as a reserve, in case we had to leave much rope behind, attached to the rocks. I saw at once that a serious question was involved, and made him give me the end. It had broken in mid-air, and it did not appear to have sustained previous injury.

'For more than two hours afterwards I thought almost every moment that the next would be my last; for the Taugwalders, utterly unnerved, were not only incapable of giving assistance, but were in such a state that a slip might have been expected from them at any moment.'

Finally they installed fixed ropes; despite this 'the men were afraid to proceed,' writes Whymper; 'and several times old Peter turned with ashy face and

'The ascent of the Matterhorn, July 14th, 1865, the fall.'
Lithograph from a drawing by Gustave Doré

124

faltering limbs, and said with terrible emphasis, "*I cannot!*"

It was not until six o'clock in the evening that the three survivors reached the snow-covered ridge of the Shoulder. From there they scrutinized the north face, but they could see no trace of their unfortunate companions. They called; there was no answering call.

"Too cast down for speech,' they collected in silence the equipment they had left on the way up. They were about to start down again when an immense arc appeared in the sky above the Lyskamm. 'Pale, colourless, and noiseless, but perfectly sharp and defined, except where it was lost in the clouds, this unearthly apparition seemed like a vision from another world; and, almost appalled, we watched with amazement the gradual development of two vast crosses, one on either side. If the Taugwalders had not been the first to perceive it I should have doubted my senses. They thought it had some connection with the accident, and I, after a while, that it might bear some relation to ourselves. But our movements had no effect upon it. The spectral forms remained motionless. It was a fearful and wonderful sight; unique in my experience, and impressive beyond description, coming at such a moment.'

I think it must have been an atmospheric phenomenon which I have witnessed three times on the Matterhorn and on Mont Blanc, and which my friend Tairraz and I were able to film. We were on the axis between a lowish sun and a background of mist (which was so also in the case of Whymper's team). On that backdrop of mist was a circle formed by the colours of the rainbow, and in the centre, the shapes of our shadows were projected. However, when we moved, our shadows moved too. This phenomenon is known by the name of 'Brocken spectre'. The atmospheric conditions necessary for its formation are quite rare and it is a singular coincidence that they occurred soon after the catastrophe.

Whymper and the Taugwalders continued the descent. Not until nightfall did they stop to bivouac. In the first hours of daylight, after 'six miserable hours' spent

on 'a wretched slab', the three men descended to Zermatt.

'Seiler met me at his door,' Whymper goes on, 'and followed me in silence to my room. "What is the matter?" "The Taugwalders and I have returned".' He did not need more, and burst into tears; but lost no time in useless lamentations, and set to work to arouse the village.'

The next day, at two o'clock in the morning, Whymper, accompanied by three English mountaineers and several guides, went to look for the bodies.

'They had fallen below as they had fallen above – Croz a little in advance, Hadow near him, and Hudson some distance behind; but of Lord Francis Douglas we could see nothing.'

Three days later the bodies were brought down to Zermatt.

'The remains of Hudson and Hadow were interred upon the north side of the Zermatt Church, in the presence of a reverent crowd of sympathizing friends. The body of Michel Croz lies upon the other side, under a simpler tomb; whose inscription bears honourable testimony to his rectitude, to his courage, and to his devotion.'

As for the survivors, the young Peter became a good guide; his father remained for a long time 'under an unjust accusation', writes Whymper. 'Nothwithstanding repeated denials, even his comrades and neighbours at Zermatt persisted in asserting or insinuating that he *cut* the rope which led from him to Lord Francis Douglas. In regard to this infamous charge, I say that he *could* not do so at the moment of the slip, and that the end of the rope in my possession shows that he did not do so beforehand.'

It seems to me pointless to dwell on this; it is quite out of the question that Taugwalder, sen., might have cut the rope.

Unfortunately, Whymper, to his discredit, fosters a doubt of another order by adding: 'There remains, however, the suspicious fact that the rope which broke was the thinnest and weakest one that we had. It is suspicious, because it is unlikely that any of the four men in front would have selected an old and weak rope when there was abundance of new, and much stronger, rope to spare; and on the other hand, because if Taugwalder thought that an accident was likely to happen, it was to his interest to have the weaker rope where it was placed.' Cowardly and insidious, these words of Whymper's, which leave one to suppose premeditation on the part of Taugwalder, sen., are worse than an explicit accusation.

Throughout this book, while 'roped' with Whymper, I have often admired him as an example of enthusiasm, frankness, boldness and decision. Here, quite suddenly, I cease to understand him: this is a posture in which I no longer recognize the character of my subject. This young man, cold and precise in character, always judicious, always self-assertive, did not beat about the bush; he did not leave to others the worry, the burden

Tomb of Michel-August Croz in the cemetery of Zermatt.
Photo: Pierre Tairraz

right-hand page
The Matterhorn seen from the Riffel Alp.
Photo: Heimhuber

pages 130-131
The south face of the Matterhorn.
Photo: Bradford Washburn

or the responsibility of choice, but made decisions, and gave his opinion even if it was not asked. It is true that he had faults, but not that one which is more serious than to accuse—to insinuate.

'I should rejoice to learn,' adds Whymper, 'that his answers to the questions which were put to him were satisfactory.' But of what value were questions put by a tribunal in the valley, when the person who was on the mountain with Taugwalder had uttered the most terrible insinuations?

Moreover, it is a curious fact that the tribunal was not to put, either to Whymper or to Taugwalder, sen.,—and perhaps the omission was deliberate—the only important question that Whymper himself has put in his book (while evading a reply to it); let us recall it: 'I found, to my surprise—indeed, to my horror—that it was the weakest of the three ropes. It was not brought, and should not have been employed, for the purpose for which it was used. It was old rope, and, compared with the others, was feeble. It was intended as a reserve, in case we had to leave much rope behind, attached to rocks. I saw at once that a serious question was involved.'

This question, to my mind, is as follows: at the Schwarzsee, at the time of taking the ropes, did Whymper, to whom they belonged, draw the attention of all his companions—guides and tourists—to them by specifying, 'this rope is strong, and can be used as a team rope; that other one is less strong, and should only be used as a fixed rope', or did he not?

If these directions were not given at the Schwarzsee, were they given later—at the camp, at the time of roping up for the ascent, at the time of roping up for the descent, or at the moment when Whymper and Hudson spoke about fixed ropes, to be installed later at the difficult passage?

If the answer is in the affirmative, Taugwalder, sen., was most gravely at fault; if it is in the negative, there was a very serious lapse of memory or piece of negligence on Whymper's part, as there was a grave forgetfulness or negligence on the part of the others concerned, in failing to ask the question.

Doubtless Whymper did not think, or even did not deem it worth while, to specify the uses to which these ropes of different thicknesses could be put: for him it went without saying, it was self-evident.

Conversely, the others doubtless thought that all the ropes were excellent.

To question 29 put by the Valais tribunal: 'In your opinion, was the rope used between Lord Douglas and yourself strong enough?' Taugwalder, sen., was to reply: 'If I had found that the rope used between Lord Douglas and me was not strong enough, I would have taken good care not to attach myself to Lord Douglas with it, and I would not have wished to put him in danger any more than myself. If I had found that rope too weak, I would have recognized it as such before the ascent of the Matterhorn, and I would have refused it.'

It is true that his reply was not entirely adequate; nevertheless, I am quite convinced of his absolute good faith. On the other hand, he seems to me to have displayed quite surprising thoughtlessness: when he had the choice between two ropes, one thick and the other thin, his reflexes did not work, he did not question himself or anyone else, but took the thin one. He could have taken the thick one – and I would add that, in my opinion, that would have made no difference to the accident.

Scientific studies have been made over about twenty years – especially since the advent of nylon ropes – on the strength of ropes, and in particular on their 'shock strength' for, in this case, that is the important thing.

If there had been no shock, that is to say, if Croz, Hadow, Hudson and Douglas had simply hung on the rope without a jerk, which would have represented a weight of about 650 lb. it is possible that even a light rope would have held. Nowadays a good 9- or 10-mm. rope has a breaking weight of 4,400 lb. It is quite a different matter when it is a case, not of weight, but of a jerk occasioned by a fall. Jerk resistance is estimated by means of a gibbet from the top of which a weight of 176 lb. is dropped. The height of free fall is 16 ft, and the jerk is registered on a fixed snap-link placed in the middle (at 8 ft). Two falls without a break are insisted upon so as to ascertain that the first is an absolute guarantee of safety. In fact, only nylon ropes of a minimum thickness of 10·5 mm. stand up to this. It is furthermore important to note that nylon ropes are relatively much stronger than hemp or manilla ones by reason of their elasticity, which absorbs a large part of the live force during a fall.

It is fair to point out that on the Matterhorn there was not a free fall through air, but a slide. Conversely, there was a chain reaction: it may be said that Hadow and Croz, falling almost simultaneously (one bringing down the other), snatched Hudson off (when the rope tautened between Hadow and Hudson), and, perhaps with the effect of the jerk, 'catapulted' him, or at least brought him away violently into space; and that the same process was repeated with even greater force for Douglas when the cord drew taut between the first three and him.

In order to determine whether the three men at the top of the team, Taugwalder, sen., Whymper and Taugwalder, jun., were to be pulled down or not, and always supposing a stronger rope between Douglas and Taugwalder, sen., everything depended on the strength of the last-named, or, more exactly, on the way he had belayed.

This was his declaration to the Valais judges: 'For greater security I turned towards the rock, and as the rope between Whymper and myself was not taut (Taugwalder, sen., in fact, was tied to two different ropes, one attaching him to Douglas and the other to Whymper), I was fortunately able to pass it round a projection of rock, which gave me the firmness needed for safety. The rope which attached me to Douglas and the others in front gave me such a shock at their fall that I am in great pain at the place where the rope was round my body.'

It may therefore be thought that:
– If Taugwalder, sen., had not passed the rope that attached him to Whymper round a rock, he himself, Whymper and young Peter would have been dragged down too.
– If the rope that connected Taugwalder, sen., to Douglas had been of normal strength for the time – and with very little elasticity, since nylon did not exist – the rope would have broken just the same under the strain not merely of the weight of four persons, but of the far greater 'shock force' due to the velocity and weight of those same persons in the course of their fall.
– Finally, if the rope connecting Taugwalder, sen., to

The Matterhorn in October. Photo: Gaston Rébuffat

133

Douglas had had the strength of a steel hawser, such that it would not break under such a 'shock force', Taugwalder, sen., would have been dragged down, and it is the rope between him and Whymper that would have broken at the level of the rock projection as a result of the jerk.

Incidentally, it is interesting again to recall that sentence of Whymper's at the beginning of his account of the descent: 'For some little distance we two (Peter and I) followed the others, detached from them, and should have continued so had not Lord Francis Douglas asked me, about 3 p.m., to tie on to old Peter, as he feared, he said, that Taugwalder would not be able to hold his ground, if a slip occurred.'

It may be thought that it was thanks to that, old Peter was saved; on the other hand, what would have been the reactions of mountaineering circles if Whymper had not been attached to the others at the moment of the accident?

It is through understanding this, and not because of any evasiveness, that I reserve my judgment on all sorts of ulterior speculations. It is always easy to advance criticisms and hypotheses after the event.

There are plenty of idiots who have talked of 'the vengeance of the Matterhorn'. There is even a phrase, 'the murderous Alp', which has found favour because it means nothing. We like to endow mountains with 'character', but at the time of an accident this is wrong. On the contrary, there are rules in all sports – in mountaineering just as in football.

On the Matterhorn, as I see it, there was not one culprit but an accumulation of errors in which each had his share; and these errors cannot just be labelled 'Hadow's incompetence' or 'an unsuitably weak rope supplied by one man and used by another', but were primarily a matter of precipitate haste and lack of system.

It would be easy to say that the catastrophe was inevitable, but it is hardly an exaggeration to claim that it was almost logically pre-ordained by the lack of cohesion with which the first ascent of the 'most inaccessible peak' was undertaken: a giddy succession of disappointments and surprises, of acrobatic compromises, or sudden improvisations, of delicate bargainings, and all this under the 'sword of Damocles', represented by the rivalry of Carrel. All the time, for every-

thing and everyone it was a case of 'take it or leave it'! Think of it: Douglas, having set off for Breuil to look for Carrel, returned with Whymper. In Zermatt, the arrival on the scene of three new and completely unexpected candidates who had all the appearance of intruders – Hudson, Croz . . . and Hadow. The innocent Hadow (the Matterhorn, the 'last great unconquered peak', was to be his second ascent – a wonderful programme!), a novice in mountaineering, inexperienced in rock-climbing, and very badly shod into the bargain; Hadow thrust upon the expedition by Hudson against all logic and all plausibility, and accepted by Whymper in order to get Croz back. But in the conduct of this enterprise, so many things were done against all logic: one second before meeting, most of these men were entirely unacquainted. For years Whymper had looked for a companion; on this day there was a crowd. From then onwards, there is nothing more to be understood: one can only try to follow. In short, everyone set out happy, but 'everyone' was too many, too many in the number of its members and the lack of common ground: except for the desire to reach the summit, there was no shared experience or common approach. And such strongly-marked and different characters! A hybrid and ill-assorted team, with two leaders, but with no one member actually bearing the responsibility. Where were the carefully thought-out plans? A train was passing, and everyone had boarded it in motion; because of Carrel, it had to move fast. No more decisions were to be taken; they did not think out action in advance, but followed it and were subject to it, each according to his temperament; they roped up, unroped and roped up again without bothering about the ropes themselves.

Carrel had been beaten. First came victory, then drama – a terrible corollary. Four deaths, and no one to blame. Yes – a trick of fate and the force of circumstance.

Whymper concluded: 'So the traditional inaccessibility of the Matterhorn was vanquished, and was replaced by legends of a more real character. Others will essay to scale its proud cliffs, but to none will it be the

mountain that it was to its early explorers. Others may tread its summit-snows, but none will ever know the feelings of those who first gazed upon its marvellous panorama; and none, I trust, will ever be compelled to tell of joy turned to grief, and of laughter into mourning . . . a momentary negligence may destroy the happiness of a lifetime. Do nothing in haste; look well to each step; and from the beginning think what may be the end.'

THE ITALIAN ARÊTE

During these days of intense joy followed by sadness on the Swiss arête and at Zermatt, what had been happening in Breuil?

After feeling sure of victory and announcing it to Sella, Giordano had to write to him to acquaint him with defeat.

Breuil, July 15th

'My dear Quintino,

'Yesterday was a bad day, and Whymper finally triumphed over the unfortunate Carrel!

'Whymper, having been reduced to despair, as I told you, by seeing Carrel moving up the mountain, tried his luck from the Zermatt side.

'Everyone here, above all Carrel, considered the climb from that side absolutely impossible. That is why we were not worried.

'On the 11th Carrel was on the mountain, and camped there at a certain height. On the night of the 11th to the 12th, and all the following day, the weather was horrible, and it snowed on the Matterhorn; on the 13th the weather was quite fine, and yesterday, the 15th, really fine.

'On the 13th little work was done; yesterday Carrel could have been at the top, and was only 500 to 600 feet away from it, when suddenly, towards two o'clock in the afternoon, he saw Whymper and the others already there.

'I had, in fact, sent a note to Carrel about Whymper's attempt, telling him that he must climb the mountain at all costs, without wasting time, and must make the route practicable; but this warning arrived too late. Added to that, Carrel did not believe an ascent from the north side was possible.

'When poor Carrel saw he had been outstripped, he no longer had the heart to carry on, and came back with all his equipment . . . He reached here just this morning.

'As you see, despite the fact that everyone did his duty, this has been a lost battle. And I am upset beyond words by it. I believe, however, that revenge would still be in order: it would be necessary to get someone to go up immediately from our side, which would at least demonstrate the feasibility of ascent by this face; Carrel still believes it possible . . .'

What, in fact, had happened up there on the Italian arête? No one knows exactly: had they lost time, either because there were too many of them or because they had had to make certain sections passable? Had a dispute arisen among the members of the team? What is certain is that Carrel, obsessed by stubborn certainty, did not believe an ascent by the Swiss arête to be possible, or, still convinced that Whymper would not find a guide to take him, did not hurry. While Whymper's team was up before dawn on the morning of July 14th, Carrel did not begin the climb until 6 o'clock; that is, with a heavy handicap. So he was only arriving at the Shoulder when Whymper reached the summit.

Despite this delay, why did he not carry on?

'He did not understand,' writes Guido Rey, 'to what extent he could still have shared in the triumph if he had continued, whatever the cost; if he had gained the summit a few hours after his rival, having, by so doing, solved the problem of the ascent of the Matterhorn by the Italian face, and if he had taken his triumph to Giordano as a gift; that would certainly have been a much more difficult victory even than the Englishman's!'

'A bad day!' writes Giordano in his notebook under the date of the 15th. 'Early in the morning Carrel came, half-dead, to tell me he had been beaten. He had counted on getting to the summit today, and believed he would be able to climb, not by way of the last turret, which he believed to be impracticable, but by way of the Zmutt slope, where there is snow.

'I decided that, in spite of everything, he at least, with a few others, should try to get to the top to plant our flag there.'

But except for Carrel, no one wanted to set out again. Giordano, who wanted to take part in the first ascent, withdrew with great self-sacrifice; nevertheless, he wished at least that the men from Valtournanche would think of their future.

'The engineer said to the guides: "Up to now I have striven for the honour of making the first ascent; fate has decided against me, I am beaten. Patience! Now, if I go to any further expense, it will be on your account, for your honour, and for your interests. Will you start again to settle the question or at least, to let there be no more uncertainty?"

'The answers were incoherent, embarrassed, thoughtless, discouraging. On leaving the Hotel Giomein for Switzerland, Mr Whymper had said: "You will never do anything with the guides of Valtournanche; they do not work for the honour, all they look for is the day's pay." What I had taken at first to be just a sudden outburst of spite, seemed to be the truth. Mr Giordano was making offers on behalf of my country which would never be made again. My country had suffered a blow to its honour, it was going to lose a fortune. I was suffering.

'So, you give up the Matterhorn! You do not want to go again. I will go myself. Who will follow me?'

Who was the man who spoke thus? It was Amé Gorret, now a priest. He had been a seminarist eight years before, and a member of the team of three, who made the first attempt on the Matterhorn and climbed the Tête du Lion.

'Jean-Antoine Carrel answered straight away: "For my part, I have not given up; if you yourself are going or if the others will come, I will start again immediately."

"Let us go, then! There are already two of us," the priest went on. "What about the others?"

' "Not I!" said one. "No more for me!" cried a second. "I would not go back if I was given a thousand francs," said a third.

' "Then there will only be the two of us, but we shall go."

'The team built itself up like that. It was around the 15th, at about midday. The rest of the day was devoted to preparations for the departure, which was fixed for the following morning, July 16th. In the evening, we had two new companions, Jean-Baptiste Bic, known as Bardolet, and Jean-Augustin Meynet, two men in the employ of M. Favre, the innkeeper.'

Giordano would still have liked to join the expedition. 'The uncertainty of the route, the difficulties that could occur in the part still unexplored and before which we had always turned back, and the changeable weather, forced us to refuse him. Carrel bluntly declared that he did not for the present feel like taking a tourist.'

'I imposed a condition on the expedition,' added the priest. 'Although deprived of the pleasure of making the ascent himself, the engineer was providing us with all the necessities. None of us, therefore, should be doing it for a daily wage; we were going of our own will, for the honour, and the vengeance of the country; I even asked that the supplies should be transported only on the first day, so that we should not be dependent on anyone until we returned, and that we should not even have the distraction of news. We should cross the Rubicon and burn our boats. My conditions were accepted.'

The next morning at four o'clock, the team was ready to go.

'After a halt at the chapel of Breuil, each one equipped, dressed and generally prepared himself in his own way. For my part I put on my hunting suit and tucked the ends of the trousers inside my stockings so that I could walk more freely. I took my beloved pointed-stick, and at half past six we set out for the climb.'

At ten o'clock they reached the Col du Lion.

'So, here was the Matterhorn in front of me,' the priest went on, 'we were going to attack it with a last supreme effort. I was very much affected and so were my companions; my heart beat hard; I could not analyse my emotions; I had palpitations; I felt I wanted to kiss this Matterhorn!'

At one o'clock in the afternoon, they arrived on the platform at the foot of the Grande Tour, and pitched camp.

' "But which route shall we take to-morrow?" asked Bic. "It seems clear enough since we have to move upwards." – "Up there, by that rock? – You'd have to be a monkey or a squirrel for that." – "We shall try." The rest of the day was spent examining the immense panorama that displayed itself beneath our eyes.'

Facing them was the Tête du Lion. Eight years ealier, Jean-Antoine Carrel, Amé Gorret, here now, accompanied by Jean-Jacques Carrel, had climbed it for the first time:

pages 138-139
The south face of the Matterhorn.
Photo: Bradford Washburn

'I was then on holiday from my seminary; this idea of climbing the Matterhorn, which made everyone smile pityingly and which was regarded as an act of lunacy, appealed to me, as well as to Jean-Antoine and Jean-Jacques Carrel. Without daring to specify the purpose of our excursion, we set out one day from the chalet d'Avouil, with a small axe to cut steps in the ice, a piece of brown bread in our pockets and a little brandy. Climbing by way of the neck of the Monthabert, we reached the Tête du Lion.

'From that time forward the ascent of the Matterhorn became an *idée fixe* with us. Carrel had his Matterhorn on the brain. As for me, I thought of it during the day, and dreamed of it at night; for me it was a nightmare. Each year saw new attempts, each attempt marked a new failure, each failure was a new provocation. The material means were lacking, and then, instead of encouragement, we met only with derision. For a few years I was unable to take part in the attempts; my time was not my own.

'At last, in 1865, I got the whole month of July for my holidays. Straight away I left for Valtournanche. On arrival, I talked to the Carrels with a view to organizing a trial climb; in the meantime, I went to greet my father, who was residing at the Col Saint-Théodule. When I came back from the col, the Carrels had just been hired by Whymper for the ascent of the Matter-horn, on the 9th and 10th of July, if the weather was good. The attempt was to be made on the Swiss side. The previous day, July the 8th, the engineer, Mr Giordano (he had come to Valtournanche to direct a systematic and final expedition), to whom the Bersagliere Carrel had been under contract for a year, arrived from Turin. Great embarrassment for Carrel. Giordano would never have wanted Carrel to fail to keep his contract with Whymper. Carrel did not want to, and could not, leave Giordano. Yet, he was tied. The weather settled the issue: it was bad.'

In the light of these words, many things become clear, and one understands better the attitude of Carrel vis-a-vis Whymper.

Now, night had fallen. 'When the weather is fine, the evenings are magnificent on the Matterhorn,' the priest goes on. 'You can see darkness rising by degrees and drowning the valleys; then, when the moon appears, you see the same valleys again, indistinctly, but at such

a depth . . . so far from you . . . you cannot understand how you come to be so high . . .'

The four men settled in a small tent; they were so tightly packed together that they did not suffer from the cold.

'On the 17th, in the morning, after having melted some lumps of ice with our spirit lamp, we had coffee, then at the entrance of the tent, we roped up, taking only the provisions that were strictly necessary, and we

Jean-Antoine Carrel. From the collection of Emile Gos

set off. The day was beautiful. The first stage, the ascent of the Tour, was difficult: the water that, when the sun shone, ran along the rocks, froze during the night; we did not know how to get a grip, even our knees were in danger of slipping, our fingers stiffened in the cold. It seemed that the sun wanted to wait until it was a bit warmer before coming out.'

In the morning, in fact, whereas the Swiss ridge, which faces north-east, is lit and warmed straight away by the first rays of the sun, the south-west Italian ridge does not get the sun until much later.

At ten o'clock, they passed the Tyndall cairn. 'We were about to set foot on unknown land; no one had ever been so far.

'It seemed natural to me to continue our ascent, as far as possible, by way of the ridge. But Carrel was struck by some slabs of rock which were redder than the rest; he thought he should go that way to reach the Swiss side. After having left on the rock where we had halted for refreshment all our supplies, except two long ropes, the one to which we were attached and another in case of unforseen circumstances, we set off again. Negotiating the col of the Shoulder was very difficult; you have to cross it by moving from one rock to another, more than three feet above, and there, form a bridge above the abyss; the rock is not always very firm. We were crawling on our bellies over the living rock, and we were about half way up the face of the Matterhorn which looks on to the Val de Zmutt, when blocks of ice and some rocks broke away from the summit and came down—a terrifying experience. After that we could see no way out. We then started to climb again by way of an almost perpendicular rock; this passage cost us the most time and effort. At length we reached the foot of the last crag which overhangs a little and we could see the blocks of ice passing above our heads without being able to reach us, and breaking themselves on the rocks that we had just climbed. Although this place was no wider than six feet, and presented a slope of at least 70°, we gave it some good names: the corridor, the gallery, the railway, etc. . . . Gripping the rocks above with our hands, we edged along this gallery.'

By way of this traverse, they were going to reach the top of the Zmutt ridge, and from there, they would easily reach the summit, but a couloir, several feet wide and up to then unseen, separated them from the ridge where they could see the 'safe and easy path'.

So, very near the goal, they were checked. 'In examining the position carefully, we noticed that at about 25 feet lower down we could get on to the ridge and thus reach the summit. Should we suspend ourselves? Yes, but where? We had not even time to fix a metal hook to the rock; we should not get out of here in daylight, and yet there were only a few more steps! This was the only remaining obstacle!'

This was the moment when he who had loved the Matterhorn so much, wished so much to climb it, had brought to it so much by his presence and his decision, was about to stay behind, in an exemplary act of generosity, so that the others could go on.

'We talked it over. I was the heaviest and the strongest. If I had been paid in gold, I could not have given up. A sacrifice was called for. I made it. Digging my heels into the ground above the abyss, my back leaning against the rock, my arms tight against my chest, I suspended two of my companions, one after the other. The third elected to stay with me. I was happy . . .'

Among the moments of egoism and bitterness, of jealousy and meanness which have so often disfigured the story of the Matterhorn, this gesture was the first that was pure and generous!

'A few minutes later, my two companions were out of danger, on an easy path. They were running. My sacrifice weighed heavily on me. Sitting astride the ridge, I was watching them, encouraging them, and with my heels I was "goading" the Matterhorn, as if to make it go, and to show it that it had been tamed: "Beast! I've got you!" I was using all my ingenuity to find a means of suspending myself in that couloir and making it practicable for tourists, when the others rejoined me; I pulled them up by the rope; they shook my hand, and after a few words of congratulation, I took my place again on the rope and off we went.'

All this is admirable in its exemplary moderation.

In the opposite direction, they followed the gallery, reached the Lion arête, arrived at the Shoulder and like Whymper and the Taugwalders three days earlier on the other side, they observed a 'phenomenon' which gave them much pleasure: 'We found ourselves in the middle of a rainbow-coloured circle; this mirage formed for all of us a sort of crown, in the middle of which we could see our shadow.'

As nightfall was not very far off, they quickly continued the descent, and at nine o'clock in the evening they arrived at the tent.

'Unable to collect drops of water, we melted a lump of ice, which we mixed with the rest of our wine; we ate our supper with a very good appetite, and, all our duties accomplished, we lay down at midnight. Rest is good after such a day. I fell into a deep sleep.

'In the morning my head was cold, and I could feel an icy weight on it. I said to Carrel:

' "What on earth have you put on my head?"

' "Nothing."

'I touched it: there was a foot of hail. The storm had come during the night; our tent was almost covered, the whole mountain was white, and the weather showed no sign of turning fine yet.

'We lost two hours melting hail for our breakfast. I had no idea that hail would be so hard to melt and would give so little water. After a poor breakfast, we left all the provisions under the tent, taking care to close it well, and, having roped up, we set off. Without Carrel, who knew this part of the mountain by heart, I do not think we could have come down then; we could not see where to put our feet or grip with our hands, and besides, everything was iced over!'

Now the difficulties of the descent were over. The four men could look towards the valley.

'From the foot of the Lion, we saw a flag floating on the Giomein–then two–then three. Our tiredness vanished; we were out of danger, and we had been seen. We all felt a shock of pleasure when we set foot on the grass again; we had hardly said a word all the time, except "Courage!", "Be careful!", "Mind how you go!",

"Look out!". I confessed to my companions that I had not dared the whole time to think whether I should ever get down. They had felt the same.

'People came to meet us. Our arrival was a triumph. At midday (July 18th) we returned to the Giomein. Only then did we learn of the disaster that had befallen the Englishmen who had been ahead of us.'

To conclude his account, the 'Mountain Bear' (for, such was the Abbé Gorret's nickname) says:

'The ascent of the Matterhorn will always be a great undertaking; but with some preparation and some work, it can be made possible for those who have a feeling for mountains and know their ways. In several places iron rings should be fixed in the rock, and ropes passed through them to which people could hold on for safety. I learn with pleasure that the Alpine Club of Turin is giving serious consideration to Canon Carrel's suggestion that a cave should be dug in the living rock at the spot called the "Cravate". By offering a safe shelter and the possibility of a halt there in bad weather, this refuge would make the ascent not only possible, but, I should say, almost easy.'

In fact, the provision of cables and huts on both sides of the Matterhorn was about to begin. There was even to be a project for a funicular railway to reach the summit! And, to borrow Abbé Gorret's word, 'cervinomania' was about to set in. But it is important to quote this sentence of Crawford Grove, who was to climb the Matterhorn in 1867:

'May the younger generation, who exult in easy victories over the once-dreaded mountain, not view with disdain the slow progress of the Alpine pioneers.'

THE RE-CONQUEST

In 1866 there were attempts on the two ridges, but no one reached the summit. From 1867 onwards, however, ascents were to start again, and even follow one another in quick succession, especially as the Italians and Swiss were to equip the Matterhorn with fixed ropes and huts (the 'Cravate' hut at 13,400 feet on the Lion arête in 1867, and a Swiss hut at 12,350 feet on the Hörnli arête in 1868) while the exploration of the mountain was to continue with the discovery of new routes. On 13 September 1867, Jean-Joseph and Jean-Pierre Maquignaz of Valtournanche climbed the terminal wall directly, thus reaching the summit by a route entirely on the Italian side. (Two years earlier, Carrel had turned this wall on the west side, which is Swiss, to reach the top of the Zmutt arête, which is also Swiss, and from there to reach the summit). Twenty days later, on October 2nd, Maquignaz brothers, achieved the first crossing from this same route, again making the direct climb where the 'Jordan ladder' was subsequently to be fixed.

On 25 July 1868, Tyndall, accompanied by the two Maquignaz brothers achieved the first crossing from Italy to Switzerland: ascent by way of the Lion arête — the summit — descent by the Hörnli arête. Six days later the same two brothers, accompanied by the porter Elie Pession, enabled F. Thioly and O. Hoiler to make the same crossing in the other direction — from Switzerland to Italy. Finally, on September 5th, the engineer Giordano, guided by the two friends and rivals Jean-Antoine Carrel and Jean-Joseph Maquignaz, reached the summit, having climbed the Lion arête. They descended by the Hörnli arête.

In 1867 a girl of eighteen, Félicité Carrel, one of the Maquignaz' team, climbed as far as the col. The Col Félicité, a small gap so named in her honour, is situated nearly at the foot of the direct route discovered by the two Maquignaz brothers. On 22 July 1871, Miss Lucy Walker became the first woman to reach the summit, by way of the Hörnli arête.

In 1876, three Englishmen, Cush, Cawood and Colgrove, were the first to climb the Matterhorn without guides; this earned them stern rebukes from *The Times*, the *Globe* and the *Saturday Review*. Finally, in 1882, Vittorio Sella, a photographer of great talent, guided by Jean-Antoine and Louis Carrel, achieved the first winter ascent of the Matterhorn on March 17th, climbing by way of the Italian arête and descending by the Swiss arête.

Meanwhile the two other arêtes of the Matterhorn, the Zmutt and the Furggen, had lured the younger generation in quest of new discoveries.

On 1 September 1879, William Penhall, accompanied by the guides Ferdinand Imseng and Louis Zurbrücken,

pages 144-145
A traverse below the Tête du Lion. The chimney and the hut. 'La grande ronde'. The Italian summit with the ropes and ladder, from Tyndall peak. From *Das Matterhorn und seine Geschichte* by Theodore Wondt

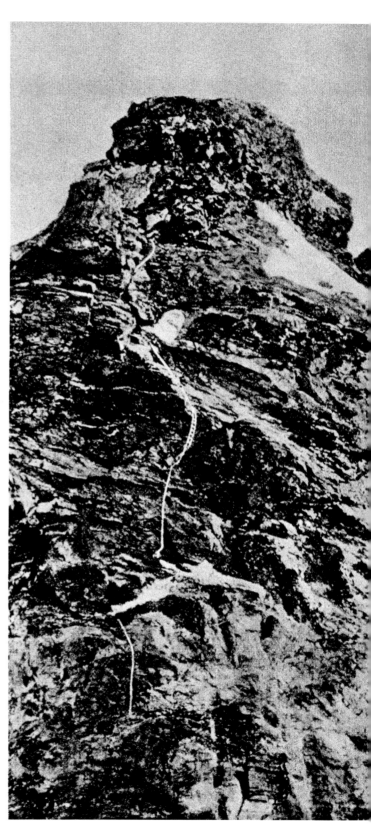

145

with a porter, left Zermatt in the middle of the night, in rather cloudy weather, in the direction of the Zmutt arête. In the morning they climbed the snow slope obliquely, reached the rocks, cut steps in very hard ice for two hours, reached the first and then the second turret, hesitated before the third because it was getting late and because the snow had been softened by the sun, and withdrew a little way to bivouac, prepared to continue the climb the following day.

Unfortunately, during the night, 'the moon, which was surrounded by a broad, bright halo at first, soon disappeared,' writes Penhall, 'the stars above the Tiefenmatten Joch became hidden, and although it was getting near the time for sunrise, the wind was growing stronger instead of dying down. When it became light, a few snowflakes were flying about and as we expected a storm, we immediately set about the descent'. Lower down, on the Zmutt glacier, 'we met Mr Mummery, who was climbing with Alexander Burgener'. And so the rivalry began.

Mummery was a young Englishman of twenty-three, full of enthusiasm; like Whymper, though with a very different character, he was to have, through his climbs and even more through his writing, an important influence on the development of mountaineering.

At the age of fifteen he climbed the Théodule, but his passion dated from childhood.

'I remember, as if it were yesterday, my first sight of the great mountain. It was shining in all the calm majesty of a September moon, and, in the stillness of an autumn night, it seemed the very embodiment of mystery.'

In 1874 he climbed the Matterhorn, 'I am aware that from that moment my interest in the peak should have ceased, that the well-conducted climber never repeats an ascent; that his object is to reach the summit, and, that object once attained, his work is over . . . . For myself, I am fain to confess a deplorable weakness in my character. No sooner have I ascended a peak than it becomes a friend, and delightful as it may be to seek "fresh woods and pastures new", in my heart of hearts I long for the slopes of which I know every wrinkle, and on which each crag awakens memories of mirth and laughter and of the friends of long ago. As a consequence of this terrible weakness, I have been no less than seven times on the top of the Matterhorn. I have

sat on the summit with my wife when a lighted match would not flicker in the windless air, and I have been chased from its shattered crest and down the Italian ridge by the mad fury of thunder, lightning and whirling snow. Yet each memory has its own peculiar charm, and the wild music of the hurricane is hardly less a delight than the glories of a perfect day. The idea which cleaves into the orthodox mountaineer that a single ascent, on one day, in one year, enables that same mountaineer to know and realize how that peak looks on all other days, in all other years, suggests that he is still wallowing in the lower bogs of Philistinism. It is true that the crags and pinnacles are the same, but this charm and beauty lies in the ever changing light and shade, in the mists which wreath around them, in the huge cornices and pendant icicles, in all the varying circumstance of weather, season, and hour. Moreover, it is not merely that the actual vision impressed on the retina reflects every mood and change of summer storm and sunshine; but the observer himself is hardly less inconstant. On one day he is dominated by the tingling horror of the precipice, the gaunt barrenness of the stupendous cliffs, or the deadly rush of the rocks when some huge block breaks from its moorings and hurtles through the air—a fit emblem of resistless wrath. On yet another day he notices none of these things; lulled by the delicate tints of opal and azure, he revels in the vaporous softness of the Italian valleys, in the graceful sweep of the wind-drifted snow, or even in the tiny flowers wedged in the joints of the granite. While the mountain may sometimes impress its mood on the spectator, as often the spectator only sees that which harmonises with his own.'

In 1879, descending from the Tiefenmatten col, Mummery discovered the west side of the Matterhorn. He studied the possibilities of an ascent, and the compelling idea of climbing it by way of the Zmutt arête was born in him.

'Having decided upon this somewhat ambitious programme, I went down to Zermatt to find a suitable guide to carry it out.'

In front of the Monte Rosa Hotel he met Alois Burgener, who gave him the 'joyful news' that his brother, Alexander, would perhaps be able to accompany him for a few days.

'The broad-shouldered Alexander, his face half

J.-J. Maquignaz. Photo: Vittorio Sella
A. F. Mummery. From *My Climbs in the Alps and Caucasus*
Alexander Burgener. From *Das Matterhorn und seine Geschichte*

pages 148-149
The Matterhorn; facing, the middle section of the Zmutt arête. Photo: Bradford Washburn

hidden in beard, was then interviewed; he bluntly expressed his opinion that to go on such an expedition with a Herr of whom he knew nothing would be a "*verfluchte Dummheit*". I was much taken by this bold expression of opinion, which appeared to me not merely indicative of a wise distrust of an untried climber, but also of a determination to drive home the attack, when once begun, to the utmost limits of possibility. My previous experience had been chiefly, if not exclusively, with men who were eager to start on any attempt, no matter how desperate, and who were far too polite to inquire whether their employer knew anything about the art of climbing. At an early stage in the proceedings, however, these men had invariably developed a most touching, but none the less most inconvenient, affection for their wives and families, and were compelled by these most commendable feelings to discontinue the ascent. The confident carriage of Alexander, and the honest outspokenness of his language, seemed to show that he was not of this sort, and to presage well for our future acquaintance.'

One day, eight years later, Burgener was to say to Mrs Mummery: 'You must go up the Teufelsgrat on the Täschorn,' In fact, on 16 July 1887, Mrs Mummery and her husband, guided by Burgener and Andermatten, achieved this difficult first ascent after sixteen hours of walking and very hard climbing almost without a halt; but on the summit a storm burst, and they had to get away with all speed. Burgener forced the pace: 'You must go on, I could a cow hold here!' were the encouraging words that Mrs Mummery heard while she was coming down pell-mell accompanied by everything underfoot.

Before starting on the great ascents, Mummery and Burgener climbed together for five days on end in order to get to know each other.

'Our campaign having been inaugurated with success, we felt ready to turn our attention to the Zmutt arête.'

But just when they were setting off, they learned that Mr Penhall with Ferdinand Imseng and Louis Zurbrücken, had left that very day to bivouac on the mountain and attack the Zmutt arête the following morning. 'We had little doubt about their success,' writes Mummery: 'The weather looked perfect, the mountain was in exceptionally good condition and the party was of most unusual skill and strength. We determined in consequence

to vary our plans and cross the Col Durand. This would enable us to watch them progress and obtain useful information for the future, and we hoped that possibly the east ridge or north-east face of the Dent Blanche would afford us consolation for the loss of the Zmutt ridge.'

The next morning, during their climb to the Staffel Alp, they observed 'that so fierce a wind was raging on the higher peaks that it seemed hardly possible any serious ascent could be effected'. Their thoughts, and also their hopes, returned immediately to the Zmutt arête, and when they met Penhall's team on its way back and learned that they had 'definitely abandoned the ridge route' Mummery and his guides decided to 'spend the day at the Stockje and see whether the wind and clouds really mean mischief'.

'On our arrival there the men soon came to the conclusion that the weather was hopeless,' Mummery goes on. 'I was, however, much too young and too eager to dream of returning, and, being wholly ignorant of all meteorological lore, I was able to prophesy fair things with such an appearance of well-founded knowledge that Burgener was half convinced. A second difficulty then arose. Our provisions were calculated on the basis of a ten hours' walk, and were obviously insufficient for a two days' campaign. Gentinetta's feelings, stimulated doubtless by the contemplation of these limited supplies, at length overcame his usual taciturnity and, unabashed by "the dignity that doth hedge" a Herr, he expressed *his* opinion of my prophecies. He backed this up by stating his conviction that at no period since the creation of the world, nor for that matter anterior to it, had such wind and such clouds resulted in aught but the most desperate and lasting bad weather. We felt that exercise would be good for his spirits, and that in any case his company would be depressing, so that he was sent back to Zermatt for extra supplies and the best man he could find to help carry them. We pointed out the place where we should camp, and undertook to intercept him on his way back should the weather appear to us too evil for sleeping out.'

Indeed, the weather seemed to be getting worse rather than better.

'Burgener's confidence began to waver, and he again suggested retiring to the Capuan luxuries of the Monte Rosa Hotel. I felt more than a tremor of doubt myself,

but the die was cast, so I trusted to luck, kept a cheerful countenance and declared that, come what might, we should have fair play from the weather. Burgener was impressed. The constant blotting out of the distant ridges, the ever gathering mass of cloud round the Matterhorn and more than a suspicion of dampness in the fierce squalls of wind that smote us at short intervals, were signs so distinct and unmistakable that he thought even a Herr must recognise them.'

Mummery recognized them; and, persistent nevertheless in his optimism, he went to rest, and even to sleep, in a corner of the hut.

'Later in the afternoon Burgener awoke me with a great thump and bid me look at the weather. My first impression was that he had come to upbraid me as an imposter, and hold up my prophecies to scorn and derision. His jubilant air and a look of thinness about the lingering clouds, however, negatived these painful thoughts, and I found that the thump was intended to convey devout appreciation of my astounding wisdom! I shook myself free from the damp rugs, and a gleam of sunshine breaking through the mists, we welcomed the returning orb of day with ear-splitting yells and a "break down" as vigorous as hobnailed boots would permit.

'The ebullitions of joy having exhausted themselves and us, we packed the knapsacks and, appropriating the store of rugs belonging to the hut, made for the rendezvous with Gentinetta.'

So Mummery and Burgener established their bivouac at the foot of the Zmutt arête.

'Having lit our fires and set the pot to boil, we sat down at the edge of the cliff overlooking the Zmutt glacier, and soon discovered Gentinetta and another man making their way rapidly through the crevasses. Meanwhile the sun had set, and with the gathering darkness the last lingering clouds dispersed as by magic. About eight o'clock the men arrived, and we found that our new recruit was Johann Petrus. We were both delighted for no bolder climber or more resolute man has ever delighted the heart of an eager Herr.'

During dinner 'Burgener and Geninetta vied with each other in extolling the weather wisdom of their Herr.'

The night was very cold: 'A keen north wind seemed to freeze us to the very marrow, and we shivered with the pain of cold under our scanty rugs. We were all glad when it was time to be moving, and at the first hint of dawn (4.15 a.m.) we began to scramble up the rocks and along the ridge leading towards the snow arête. At 5.20 a.m. we reached its foot, and on a sheltered ledge found the debris of Penhall's camp.'

The four men made a halt for breakfast; then, making use of the steps cut by Penhall's team, they climbed rapidly up the ridge and reached the Dents de Zmutt.

'Beyond the third tooth we were pulled up by a deep cleft . . . . . Further direct progress was impossible, as the ridge rose perpendicularly above them. For another three-quarters of an hour we examined it without being able to see a satisfactory way across, and unpleasant doubts were being freely expressed when a distant jodel attracted our attention. Far away down the mountain we espied three dots, whom we at once and rightly guessed to be Penhall and his guides.'

The arrival of the Penhall party spurred Mummery and his guides on: they advanced as far as the spot where the 'evil slope' had to be tackled. 'The discussion was once more renewed,' Mummery continues. 'Burgener was distinctly averse to attempting it, but as there was no other way, Petrus went forward to explore.

'I have not the slightest doubt that Bergener's objection to this slope was exclusively due to the fact that we had never previously been together in this sort of work. It was obviously practicable, but it was equally obvious that the slip of one meant the destruction of all who were roped to him. Subsequent experience enables me to sympathize with his feelings. The knowledge that you can do nothing to arrest a slip, combined with a lively fear that one may occur, creates as unpleasant a situation as it is easy to imagine. The fear of slipping oneself is almost a delight when compared with the trap-like feeling induced by the rope with an "unknown quantity" at the end of it.

'Our halts at this point and on the third tooth had exceeded two hours, and we had no more time to lose. Petrus seemed to be getting on all right, so Burgener made ready for the traverse. Though by no means a big man in the valley, on an ice-glazed slope he seems to visibly dilate, and looks like a veritable giant when wielding his resistless axe. For some reason, probably to get a decent excuse for unroping Gentinetta and saving him from the risk of the "unknown quantity", Burgener told us to pay him out till he should be

"*ganz fest*". We paid out a hundred feet of rope, and as there was no immediate prospect of his being '*ganz fest*', and as in the event of a slip it was tolerably certain it would make no difference whether he were or no, I cautiously followed his track; Gentinetta bringing up the rear, free from the dangerous entanglement of the rope. Having traversed in all about a hundred and fifty feet we were able to turn up the slope, and soon reached firm rock, which, though very steep, offered good hold and plenty of it. Burgener dashed up at a furious pace. Suddenly a splinter of rock caught his coat, and an agonized yell told us that his pipe, his faithful companion on many a hard-fought climb, and the gift of his most trusted Herr, had been jerked out of his pocket and had plunged down to the Matterhorn glacier.'

The party regained the arête, and as soon as it began to overhang, climbed obliquely towards the right, on the west face.

'Burgener anxiously scanned the huge cliff and then gripped my hand and exclaimed, "The pipe is avenged, we are on the summit," which I took to mean that we should be there sometime.

'Burgener having borrowed Gentinetta's pipe – which by the way, he did not return till we got back to Zermatt – we began the ascent of the western face. We traversed a short distance and then turned straight up over slabby, icy and somewhat loose rocks. They were not, however, difficult, and we made rapid progress. Probably we should have done better still further to the right, but Burgener was very properly averse to this course, as he thought it might bring us too directly above the other party. Even where we were, he insisted on the utmost care to avoid upsetting stones.'

They soon reached the level of Carrel's Corridor, regained the Zmutt arête, and arrived at the summit at 1.45 p.m. 'The day was perfectly calm and the view cloudless. Time fled swiftly, and when Burgener came to me with the rope at 2.30 p.m. I could hardly believe we had been three-quarters of an hour on the summit.' The four men set off, and descended by the 'chain-clad' Hörnli arête, from which they saw Penhall's party reaching the top of the Zmutt arête.

They rapidly continued the descent. 'Great care was required to avoid the broken glass and sardine boxes which had accumulated in large quantites.' After a

short halt we see them hurrying down without difficulty towards the Zmutt glacier; at seven in the evening they arrived at Zermatt.

That same day, 3 September 1879, another great first ascent had been achieved on the Matterhorn. It will be remembered that on September 1st and 2nd, Penhall and his guides Imseng and Zurbrücken, had made a serious attempt on the Zmutt arête. After a very uncomfortable bivouac, repulsed by all the omens of bad weather, they had turned back and descended to Zermatt, passing Mummery's team on the glacier.

'Yet the storm seemed to think better of it, did not burst, but passed off,' Penhall writes. 'At about six o'clock Imseng came up to me and said very seriously that Zurbrücken had just been to consult the priest, and the opinion of that worthy was that it would be fine the following day, and – "would I like to start again after the *table d'hôte?*" I confess I should hardly have proposed it myself, but as *he* suggested it, I agreed.'

Penhall and his two guides, men of extraordinary endurance, left Zermatt at ten o'clock at night: 'We were all half asleep and the events of the two previous days seemed like a dream.'

At three-thirty they reached the rocks, and at about five o'clock they were at the edge of the great gully that falls almost sheer from the Dents de Zmutt and cleaves the left part of the west face. First they climbed the rocks on the right side of the gully, and at the place where it is narrowest, they crossed it to get to the other side, where they found 'that the rocks were smooth and much steeper' – but they were firm.

In fact, this gully, since christened 'Penhall's Gully', gives the general line of ascent; it is not itself climbed, however, for it is extremely dangerous because it canalises all the stone-falls.

At one moment Penhall saw Mummery 'on the arête just at the highest point we had reached two days before'.

Then the climb was resumed: 'About one and three-quarter hours from the point where we crossed the

The west face of the Matterhorn; right, Tête du Lion and Lion arête; left foreground, the Zmutt arête; far left, the north face and Hörnli arête.
Drawing by Pierre Bichet

couloir we found ourselves standing on a narrow ledge of rock just below a small precipice which there was no possibility of ascending. Although we were conscious that every minute was of the utmost value, we were here compelled to call a halt in order to decide upon the direction of our further advance.'

Though nothing was said, the race betwen the two Englishmen was on, with Mummery on the arête, off to a good start, and Penhall on the rock-face.

Deterred by the wall looming above them, Penhall and his guides tried to turn the right flank of the obstacle. Unhappily, after three-quarters of an hour they were only about a hundred feet higher, and, having conversed 'rather with blank looks than audible words', they decided to retrace their steps. This was more easily said than done:

'Any attempt to describe the events of the hour which followed would be pure waste of time. Many of my readers must have been in similar positions, and their memories will assist them in picturing to themselves what language is unable to convey. By those who do not know what slopes of this kind are like, any endeavour to give an idea of our position would be at once dismissed as incredible.

'For one hour and five minutes we were forced to descend with the utmost care, each being obliged to devote his whole attention to himself and give up all idea of assisting his companions.

'At last we found ourselves once more on the ledge we had so unfortunately abandoned, with considerable diminution of flesh at the end of our fingers, and two hours of valuable time lost.'

The only answer was to try towards the left.

'On starting again we got on better than we had anticipated for the first half-hour, when suddenly we came upon a fresh and unexpected difficulty; the rocks were no longer wet, but covered with a thin coating of ice. They would not have been particularly easy under the best of circumstances, and with this additional complication required the greatest caution. Fortunately this did not last long, and we were soon standing on a narrow strip of snow that we had not noticed before. The appearance of the upper part of the mountain changes constantly; from this point we were amazed at the size of the crags above us to our left.'

But from now on, they were happy, and they deserved

to be: 'The rest of our way was clear, there was nothing to prevent us from getting to the part of the face at which the Italians must have traversed it in their first ascent. So on we went over the same sort of smooth rocks, of which we had already had so much.'

In fact, they came to the upper part of the Zmutt arête, and the beneficent rays of the sun spilling over the summit suggested to them the idea of a short halt.

'Though not sorry to sit down, we were restless to get really to the top, particularly when a shout from the shoulder told us the other party were rapidly descending.' Half an hour later, at three o'clock in the afternoon, Penhall and his guides reached the summit. 'It was not unpleasantly cold, so having considerably lightened the knapsacks and wine tin, we enjoyed the view for a good half-hour.' Then they went to the Swiss summit and began the descent. Penhall was surprised to find that 'the number of ropes above the shoulder had been largely increased. In one place there were three ropes and a rusty chain all together'. and he adds: 'Let us try and keep one side of the Matterhorn at any rate for those who really admire the most wonderful mountain in the Alps and who like to climb it for its own sake, and then we can give up the other arêtes to be decorated, if necessary with chains and ladders from top to bottom, and so formed into the cockneys' high road from Breuil to Zermatt.'

Almost at a run, Imseng, Zurbrücken and Penhall pressed on to Zermatt, which they reached at 9.45.

'Refusing to answer any questions till the following morning, we went off to bed, and I confess for my own part I could scarely keep awake while I undressed. This was hardly to be wondered at. Penhall and his guides had slept for two hours on Sunday night, not at all on the arête on Monday night, and they had climbed throughout the night from Tuesday to Wednesday and the whole day, almost without a stop.

right-hand page
The Zmutt arête on the Matterhorn.
Photo: Bradford Washburn

pages 156-157
The upper part of the south face of the Matterhorn: left, the Lion arête; top left, the Italian summit; right, the Furggen arête; top right, the Swiss summit.
Photo: Bradford Washburn

'What a night's rest in the Alps will do is wonderful, but I was disgusted when, on looking out at nine o'clock next morning, I saw my guides sitting on the wall, as if they had been up hours.' It is fair to point out that Zurbrücken and, in particular, Ferdinand Imseng were guides of the very first order, with extraordinary powers of endurance.

That same year, 1879, the first Swiss hut, known as 'the old hut', was abandoned: it had become too small and was letting in the rain. In 1880, Alexander Seiler and the Swiss Alpine Club which had financed the first, had another built, with the aid of the commune of Zermatt, at a height of 10,700 feet, at the foot of the Hörnli arête.

On the Italian side, it was in 1885 that the Italian Alpine Club built the Grande Tour hut, at about 13,000 feet, to replace the Cravate shelter; it was rebuilt in 1891, and it was in 1905 that the Turin section of the Italian Alpine Club built the Luigi Amedeo di Savoia hut, in memory of the Duke of Abruzzi, at 12,600 feet, which is still in use today.

Finally, in 1916, thanks to the generosity of the Belgian industrialist Ernest Solvay, a little hut was built at 13,000 feet on the Hörnli arête.

As for the fixed ropes, there is often talk of taking them away to restore to the Matterhorn its pristine beauty; in fact, they only increase, in quantity and length. So in our time, the climb is considerably easier than in the time of Whymper and Carrel, and even of Mummery and Penhall.

In 1879, then, there were four routes to the summit of the Matterhorn; the Hörnli arête, the Lion arête, the Zmutt arête and the west face by way of the Penhall Gully. There remained one arête and three faces for bold climbers with a passion for first ascents.

The first to be tackled was the fourth arête, the Furggen arête, which in 1880 became the order of the day.

'A year later,' Mummery writes, 'at Couttet's Hotel, I was dreaming peacefully of my *bien aimée* the Aiguille des Charmoz – whom we had successfully wooed the previous day – when Burgener broke in upon my slumbers and ejected me, ruthlessly, from the soft comfort of my bed.

'Protests were in vain. The huge ridge of the Furggen Matterhorn had long tempted his desires. All the ingrained fighting instinct was aroused in him. He wished to hurl himself once more at the cliffs and ridges, matching his skill against their dumb, passionless resistance, and forcing them now, as ever, to yield to his reckless onslaught.'

Mummery and Burgener, as well as Venetz, who was with them, immediately left Chamonix, arrived at Stalden at four in the afternoon and spent the night there. 'By so doing, Burgener and Venetz were enabled to make those ecclesiastical arrangements which the peculiar enormity of the Furggen ridge seemed to render desirable. Such elaborate and careful preparations appeared to me a trifle uncanny, and subsequent events showed very clearly the evil effects which this sort of indulgence in religious festivities has upon the nerves. However, both Burgener and Venetz appeared to be in excellent spirits when they returned, and we whiled away the summer evening with stories of chamois hunting and the great deeds wrought amongst the winter snow.'

It is perfectly true that mountaineering consists of making ascents, first ascents if one so wishes, but it also consists of evenings spent together with one's climbing companions. What pleasure it would have been that evening to listen to Burgener and Venetz in the company of Mummery!

The time for departure for a first ascent comes quickly, and the next day, at three-quarters of an hour past midnight, the three men left the Monte Rosa Hotel at Zermatt, and climbed, at dead of night, 'to the level stretch of boggy ground, under the Schwarzsee'. The tragi-comedy was about to begin: 'A few minutes later we were surrounded by the weird, unearthly flicker of innumerable will-o'-the-wisps,' writes Mummery. 'At every step they floated away on either hand, yet, seemingly, no sooner had we passed, than they crept up stealthily behind, dogging our footsteps with a cruel vindictiveness from which there appeared no hope of escape or flight.

'The men were horror-struck. Burgener gripped my arm and hoarsely whispered – "*Sehen Sie, Herr, die*

Looking down from the Furggen arête. Photo: A. Cicogna

159

todten Leute!"

'I am fain to confess, the crawling bluish flames, the utter silence, and the contagion of my companions' superstitious fear, thrilled me with instinctive horror. I perceived, however, that if we were not to return to Zermatt baffled and beaten a second time, the delights of a spiritualistic séance must be abandoned in favour of a matter-of-fact explanation.

'However, Burgener and Venetz were not to be easily convinced.

'"*Ach lieber Herr*, did you not see the war.dering light on the Gorner glacier? There is no boggy ground there. That *was* a Geist!"

'In vain I protested that it was a lantern. "A lantern! What could anyone want there? It was on the road to nowhere; besides, it did not move forwards like a lantern, but kept wandering to and fro, twinkling and dodging, precisely as a disembodied spirit, with no particular business on hand, might be expected to do."

'The position was serious enough in all conscience. It is a well ascertained fact (attested by all the ecclesiastical authorities of the Saas, Zermatt, and Anzasca valleys) that anyone seeing a "Geist" is certain to be killed within twenty-four hours! I pointed out to Burgener that this being so, there could be no advantage in turning back, for, either they were ghosts, in which case we must be killed, or they were not ghosts, in which case we might as well go on. The men admitted the dilemma, but suggested that even so, climbing up a peak for the purpose of being chucked off it by mischievous "Geister" is not pure and unalloyed joy. I readily assented to this proposition, but pointed out the inconvenience and discomfort, both mental and bodily, of being haled from the Monte Rosa Hotel, perhaps from the very *table d'hôte* itself, by the foul fiend and his myrmidons . . . . Being the most sceptical of the party, I was allotted the post of leader.' But their difficulties were not over: 'Suddenly in the distance, appeared two lights, "The other parties!" I exclaimed, thinking the men's fears would be somewhat allayed by company. But Burgener and Venetz had "Geister" on the brain, and vowed that these also were undoubted specimens of that genus. I urged them to force the pace and find out. "What!" cried they, "do you know so little of Geister as to attempt such a thing as that?" Burgener, after much persuasion,

consented to jodel, a proceeding attended with very grave danger—"Geister" don't like being jodelled at—and only to be effected in doubtful and tremulous sort. To our delight, however, back came a cheery yell, that the men recognized as belonging to Peter Taugwalder.

'The sceptics in the party being much strengthened by this most opportune support, we pushed onwards more cheerily.

'As the sun rose, its earliest beams fell on long wisps of snow torn from the crest of the Matterhorn, and though of fairy-like beauty, suggestive of more wind than we quite cared for.'

They arrived at the base of the glacier which is at the foot of the east face of the Matterhorn, lost some time among the séracs, then by way of a steep gully above the Breuiljoch they climbed beyond the lower spur, reached the aréte, swiftly scaled the easy part, and at nine in the morning reached 'the great tower, seen from Zermatt on the left sky-line just beneath the final peak'. From that moment everything went badly. The clouds spun around the mountain, 'the roar of each furious gust being followed by the ominous clatter of broken icicles, and the crash of great stones torn from the summit rocks'. Moreover, 'The final peak looked very formidable, and, in such weather, could not have been assailed with any reasonable approach to safety. We resolved, in consequence, to traverse on to the ordinary Hörnli route.' Nevertheless, this long traverse had to be made beneath falls of rock and blocks of ice that the storm was tearing from the upper faces . . . . 'After more than one extremely narrow escape, we reached a point somewhat sheltered by a projecting crag above . . . . Burgener—who has a most proper and prudent objection to every form of waste—suggested that it would be well to drink our Bouvier, and consume our other provisions, before any less fitting fate should overtake them. The knapsack was accordingly unpacked, and, in the grave and serious mood befitting the solemnity of the occasion, we proceeded to demolish those good things with which the thoughtful Seiler had stored our bags. Under these various benign influences our spirits rose rapidly, and Burgener's face resumed its wonted look of confidence.'

Finally Burgener, Mummery and Venetz got to the Hörnli arête at the level of the Shoulder, and by way of it quickly reached the summit.

'We should have been in Zermatt by 5 p.m. had I not made an unlucky remark concerning Geister and Todten Leute. These good (or bad?) people had been forgotten amidst the excitement of the climb, but my unlucky remark awakened Burgener to the imminence of the catastrophe that must necessarily overtake us . . .

'We descended with the utmost elaboration of care, only one moved at a time, and constant entreaties were even then required before rope enough was paid out to enable anybody to move. These elaborate precautions were backed up by a great profusion of pious (and some-times the reverse) ejaculations, and we each vowed a candle of peculiar splendour and size to a saint of Burgener's acquaintance, subject, of course, to the provision that the said saint enabled us to baffle the malignant Geister. When we duly arrived on the Furggen glacier, Venetz suggested a doubt as to whether the saint had really earned the candles. He showed us a small necklet he was wearing, which contained the tooth or thumb-nail, or other decaying debris, of an exceptionally holy saint, and which, he averred, was, as cricketers would say, "quite able to lick all the Zermatt Geister off its own bat". However Burgener assured me that, in bargains of this sort, it is always the better plan to pay, "especially", he added, "when a few francs are alone at issue". So we subsequently duly discharged our debts. We got back to Zermatt just in time for *table d'hôte*, after a day of the most varied interest and excitement.'

It is certain that, over and above the pleasure of the climb, these ascents in the company of the extraordinary Burgener must have been as heart-warming as they were picturesque. However, the Furggen arête had been only partially climbed; it was not to be completely climbed until sixty-one years later.

*

In the meantime the Matterhorn was often to be the setting for remarkable adventures.

The most outstanding was without a doubt that of two Austrians: Professor Guido Lammer and his com-panion August Lorria, on 13 August 1887.

'I was resolved,' writes Lammer, 'to attempt the impossible and never let slip an opportunity to risk my life. I was a powerful fellow, full of wild ardour, and a true son of that era in which the March storms of a spiritual renaissance were raging.

'I was not immoral, but amoral, like the oak or the eagle or the storm. We acknowledged no other principle than the free manifestation of the personality according to the profoundest laws of its nature.

'As with my emergent philosophy, so my moun-taineering projects and enterprises knew absolutely no moral barrier.'

Later, Lammer continues: 'I was shot through with a current of demoniac forces, I was myself all demon; good sense and moral feelings remained powerless to restrain me. If we were due to be the victims of a catastrophe that summer, it was because it was written in the stars. For is it not in your heart that shine the stars of your destiny?'

Lammer and Lorria climbed to the derelict Stockje hut, facing the west wall of the Matterhorn that they wanted to climb. 'I have never seen or heard such formidable stone-falls as at that season on the Matter-horn,' Lammer writes. A few hours earlier in Zermatt, Burgener had warned him about the avalanches, and had advised him to choose the Zmutt arête. 'I remained deaf to his advice: the impetuous torrent of my desires rushed onwards, discounting all obstacles.'

At about one o'clock in the morning the two men got up, and shortly afterwards they plunged into the silent night. The cold had taken possession of the mountain wall; until the sun returned to warm it again, the rocks would stay imprisoned in the ice.

The two men at first climbed by way of the rocks on the right side; then came the moment to traverse the gully: 'I had never before seen such a deep avalanche course: even with my hand raised I could not reach the edge.'

Lammer nevertheless succeeded in getting out of it and reaching the rock-slabs of the left bank: 'We reached

pages 162-163
The west face of the Matterhorn. Left, background, side-view in shadow, the north face. Left foreground, the Zmutt arête. Facing, the west side. Right, Tête du Lion, Col du Lion and Lion arête; Tyndall Peak.
Photo: Bradford Washburn

163

the west wall, and it was then that Destiny opened its bloody jaws.'

Indeed, conditions were very bad: the wall was almost entirely covered with verglas. Anyone else, without a doubt, would have turned back, but Lammer did not give up: 'I went barefoot, and in this way slid between patches of verglas for whole hours; as for Lorria, he had to wait until I could pull him with the aid of the rope. When there were strips of snow, in my bare feet I set about cutting steps so as not to lose time, and I hardly suffered from the cold.

'We struggled in this way for more than seven hours, and things went from bad to worse. At one in the afternoon we were only at the level of the teeth of the Zmutt spur, and as the verglas was getting worse hour by hour, we realized clearly that we would get through neither that day nor the next, but only after a week of complete thaw . . .

'Furious, and with my heart boiling with vexation, I retraced my steps. In a desperate hand-to-hand struggle we cautiously climbed down those slopes, which were steep enough to make one shudder. At that moment the burning sun from the south-west finally burst all the bonds of hell, the icy chains were shattered, and clashed together deafeningly, and it would be impossible to imagine a more terrifying uproar. Black masses the size of farm carts broke away and tumbled down with a noise of thunder, leaping three hundred feet, rebounding on rock projections, and then flying into a multitude of pieces which rent the air, whistling and flying off on unpredictable paths. One of us continually looked upward while the other was climbing down, and at the shout of alarm we flattened our trembling bodies tightly against the rock, whose protection was nevertheless doubtful on those slabs.'

Shortly after four in the afternoon the two men at last arrived at the place where they had to cross the gully, and Lammer put his boots on again.

'Every five minutes, and even more often, one of these sinister convoys came roaring past; for all the rocks and masses of snow that fell or slipped in the vicinity of our gigantic funnel could only sweep down that single gully.'

' "Let's bivouac on the wall itself!" said Lorria.

'I was seized by a fit of wild arrogance,' Lammer went on. 'After a successful climb, perhaps, but after a defeat, never! Lorria opposed me with commonsense arguments, but I was the stronger, I was passion, I was defiant anger, I was the all-powerful voice, I was the demon. I? No! And Lorria yielded – to his misfortune.'

So they went down the gully!

'So that our progress would be quicker, Lorria was obliged to run without taking precautions, while I, planted deeply in the névé, paid out the firmly-held rope from my bent right leg over my obliquely-placed left thigh. Then it was my turn to slide after him as quickly as possible in the snow, which formed into a ball: I felt myself to be a master in the art of the glissade. The rocks continued to hail above our heads, but they were rarer and smaller than those which had threatened us on the wall higher up and more to the south. If only we were already on the far side of the gully! Only a few feet as the crow flies separated us from the edge, and safety. But each time we were ready to risk the devilish traverse of the avalanche gully, a black and white salvo of snow and masses of rock crackled down, sweeping the deadly abyss from top to bottom . . .

'The catastrophe happened in a commonplace way, not at all dramatically,' Lammer continues. 'We had long since given up turning to keep an eye on the falling rock, reckoning that the precaution was useless and demanded too much time, and we were simply committing ourselves to the mercy of destiny. Suddenly, however, I looked up: a tiny avalanche was swooping down on me, perhaps one of those waves of snow that I had brought down with me at the outset, and had immediately stopped out of consideration for Lorria. In another moment I would have buried my ice-axe deep in the névé and held back the whole mass with all the strength of my chest. But already the treacherous mass was dragging the half-melted snow away from under my feet with ease; already losing my balance, I thrust with my ice-axe, but it went through the snow like butter, without meeting any resistance, and the avalanche, on which I was outstretched, thus increased in volume, rushed in the direction of Lorria, who was immediately hurled into the dreaded abyss.

'During this horrible flight my mind remained completely clear, and I can tell you, my friends: that is a fine way to die. "*Paetus, it does not hurt!*" A pin-prick hurts more than a fall. No more deadly frights or fits of moral anguish. Only at the beginning. Once my last efforts to save myself had proved themselves vain, a great feeling of resignation took possession of me. The man who was thrust into that narrow channel, who was flung violently on to the soft body of his companion, and then, by the jerk of the rope, snatched sharply back into the clear air – that man was a stranger. An unfeeling piece of wood. My "self" hovered above the whole incident, like some calm, curious spectator at a circus.' Lammer goes on, very seriously: 'Only one thing troubled me: that sun full in my face – it was about half past five – which, through that swirling cloud of snow, was blinding me so much that I had to shut my eyes.'

The avalanche came to a halt at the bottom of the gully. 'The roaring of the cataract died away, the hiss of the avalanche ceased. I opened my eyes, and a *boundless astonishment* seized me: *no relief, no feeling of gratitude, no regret.* I found myself sitting at the top of a mound of lumps of snow and rock, alone in that fearful solitude: the rope tied round me ran down into the snow. Only then was I shaken by nervous shudders; swiftly, I pulled on the rope and, clearing the snow away from it with my feet, I followed it . . . from the snow emerged the greenish, bloodstained face of a corpse. Thin trickles of blood came from a huge lump above his eye and oozed into his mouth. The rope was twisted twice round his neck. I drew my knife and cut it instead of untying it, and likewise I took off his rucksack, as if that might bring him back to life. Then I shook him and called his name, stammering. I spoke to him in a voice of entreaty, I tried to make him understand, I set him on his feet, but he uttered a great cry of pain and fell backwards . . .'

'Our situation,' Lammer continues, 'was still extremely critical.' In their fall, the two men had passed over the two bergschrunds, they had lost their ice-axes, their hats and their goggles. They were at the top of the avalanche cone, the rocks continued to fall with undiminishing violence. Lammer was bleeding, he had countless wounds on his hands that went as deep as the joints, he had a broken nose and a broken right ankle, as he was to discover later. However, they had to get down at all costs to avoid being slaughtered by the rocks. Lammer let himself slide, and dragged Lorria after him by sheer strength. Lorria cried out and tried to cling 'convulsively to the masses of hard snow', but Lammer pulled him and dragged him on to the level part of the glacier as far as the last piece of rock, where he made him as comfortable as he could. "I no longer had the strength to carry him further,' writes Lammer, 'so I put my thick loden coat over him, pulled my dry woollen stockings on to his hands and placed my rucksack under his feet. Should I tie him to the rock? I did not do so; it seemed to me inhuman and pointless. There were no crevasses anywhere near.'

It was six o'clock in the evening when Lammer set off to look for help. He had to avoid the crevasses whose fragile snow bridges were considerably softened by the sun. He hoped to find someone at the old Stockje hut, but there was no one there, and he had to set off again for Zermatt by first descending the tongue of the Zmutt glacier.

'Soon my injured foot refused to walk or to limp. I began to crawl like a caterpillar. I was so weak and exhausted that I often made no attempt to avoid the pools of water, but simply went through them.' In the moraines he lost his way and crawled in all directions for hours. 'Instead of using my raw and painful hands, I took the weight on my elbows. At one moment I fell into a twilight state of consciousness – or did I faint? But a fierce "I must" snatched me out of it, and I continued to drag myself eastwards.'

At last, towards midnight, when he had reached a high crest of the moraine, he was obliged to stop. 'In my distress and despair, I lay on my back, my face bloodstained. I raised my eyes to the zenith towards the gentle, green Déeneb and let them lose themselves in the soft, divinely beautiful night. O cruel and magnificent Matterhorn, bathed in the liquid silver of the moon, everything around is radiant with a white light; only on me do you cast your shadow, only me do you rob of direction and sight! And yet, O cruel mountain, our conqueror, O cruel nature, O unfeeling god, I love you in all your merciless beauty, in your granite indifference. I, the indestructible one, am a match for you.'

At one o'clock in the morning Lammer knocked at the door of a Staffel Alp shepherd's chalet. A woman went down to Zermatt with a message for Seiler. As for Lammer, he fell into a deep sleep.

At six in the morning the rescue party arrived. Lammer explained where he had left Lorria. 'At eight o'clock the rapid climbers found Lorria; in his delirium he had almost completely undressed and had rolled in the snow.'

This extraordinary exploit was the act of an exceptional personality, but it is representative of an era and perhaps of an attitude of mind. It is in the same class as the feats of Saussure, Whymper, Mummery and Guido Rey.

The way Professor Lammer tackled the Matterhorn was quite appalling, and it was clear from the outset that a conventionally successful climb – I do not mean by that an easy climb – would have disappointed him. His energy was extraordinary, but the use he made of it, except when it was a matter of rescuing his companion, was quite unproductive and sometimes ridiculous – climbing barefoot in the snow, for instance. He was doubltess constantly at pains to prove to himself that he existed and that nothing could stop him.

At the moment when they decided to turn back, it is very probable that he and Lorria could without exceptional difficulty have reached Zermatt arête, which was surrounded 'still with mystery', as he put it, but about which, as he mentions, he had spoken to Burgener. But in doing so he would have denied himself the descent under the avalanches which, he knew, would not be long in coming, and from which he was looking forward to an 'experience' rich, to his way of thinking, in many ways.

Lammer wore his heart on his sleeve, and it was no ordinary heart; but it could be that in wanting to show too much, and to prove too much, he consciously or unconsciously exaggerated on more than one occasion. This he did unfortunately without the slightest touch of humour.

'One of my feet,' Lorria was to say later, 'was broken, and both were cemented into the snow and had to be freed with an ice-axe . . . The descent of the glacier to Staffel Alp was a terrible affair . . . At eight o'clock in the evening I was taken to Zermatt, to the Monte Rosa Hotel, where I remained unconscious, with my life in the balance, for twenty-one days.'

Nevertheless, as Lammer pointed out: 'Thanks to his strength, Lorria recovered from this fourteen-hour bivouac and from his cerebral disturbance. Only his left foot remained disabled.'

In a quite different context, the death of Jean-Antoine Carrel at the foot of the mountain which had witnessed his birth was grand and noble.

On 23 August 1890, the 'Bersagliero' set out once again to climb the Matterhorn which he had conquered by way of the Italian arête twenty-five years earlier. Two days before, at Courmayeur, while he was descending Mont Blanc, a young student from Turin, Leone Sinigaglia, met him and engaged him. Carrel thought that the fearful storm of the 18th (a storm during which Jean-Joseph Maquignaz disappeared on Mont Blanc with Antoine Castagneri and Count Umberto de Villapiana, but no one knew anything about this yet) would have left no traces on the Matterhorn, and that the fine weather which had returned would last a few more days.

In Breuil, a second guide, Charles Gorret, the abbé's brother, was engaged, and on the 23rd, at 2.15 in the morning, the three men left the valley under a magnificently starry sky with the idea of crossing the Matterhorn in a single day, climbing by way of the Lion arête and descending by the Hörnli arête.

However, the rocks of the Col du Lion were still covered with verglas, and it was not until half-past ten that they reached the Grande Tour hut. It was too late to contemplate continuing the long crossing; prudence advised waiting a day.

Carrel, being a little weary, took the opportunity to take a nap. Two hours later, when he awoke, the weather was changing. It was bad in the west; the horizon was ringed with black, menacing clouds. At three in the afternoon the four Valtournanche guides, three of the Maquignaz family and one Bich, who had inspected the ropes on the Italian arête that morning, and whom Sinigaglia, Carrel and Gorret had found at the hut, took advantage of a bright period to descend. Carrel and his companions could wait, since they did not wish to climb the Matterhorn until the following day. But the weather worsened very rapidly. At the end of the day the storm burst with extreme violence: squalls of hail and snow, and peals of thunder which shook the little hut moored to its cables.

'I recall,' writes Sinigaglia, 'that the air was so saturated with electricity that for two hours at a stretch the night was strangely luminous, and one could see in the hut as if it had been daytime.' The whole night, the

The Hörnli arête. Photo: Pierre Bichet

following day, and again the night after, the storm continued to rage without a lull. The cold was so intense that they had to burn everything, including the benches in the hut, to get a little warmth. Provisions began to run short: 'The situation became disquieting,' writes Sinigaglia. 'The hurricane which raged continuously had put us into a state of tension which was hard to bear. It had snowed and hailed all the time, the rock was in the worst possible condition, and we feared that if we stayed longer and the storm went on, we would find ourselves cut off for several days in the hut.'

On the morning of the 23rd the weather was still terrible, but as the wind had abated somewhat, they decided to try the descent.

At nine they left the hut, but the weather and the conditions were so fearful that it took them five and a half hours to reach the Col du Lion. The ropes were frozen, the rocks were completely iced over, and on top of that, fresh snow had covered everything.

At the Col du Lion, where they had been hoping for a lull the storm redoubled its fury. 'We had constantly to scrape the ice away from our eyes . . . it was almost impossible to speak or communicate in any way,' Sinigaglia continues. 'Nevertheless, Carrel continued to direct the descent in admirable fashion, with unfailing coolness and energy, and with supreme skill . . . I was amazed to see him in such form. Gorret backed him up splendidly. We came upon unforeseen difficulties and, in places, indescribable dangers; especially as the blizzard led Carrel off course in spite of his thorough knowledge of the Matterhorn.'

Covered with snow, carpeted with verglas, the 'Great Staircase' had become a gigantic succession of springboards. At eleven o'clock at night they were still on their way down. 'We kept going because it was impossible to stop,' writes Sinigaglia. 'Carrel, by a marvellous instinct, at last discovered the passage by which we had gone up, and we took a minute's halt to swallow a mouthful of brandy . . . Shortly afterwards, in the middle of a névé,' Sinigaglia goes on, 'we saw Carrel slowing down; then he slipped and fell two or three times. Gorret asked him what was the matter, and he replied: "Nothing!" But he moved only with difficulty from then onwards. Gorret, putting this weakness down to the exhausting descent, then took over the lead, and Carrel seemed to be better after this change. He walked well, though

with a kind of slowness that was not usual with him.'

They had almost completed the descent. Gorret, who was going down first, was only a few steps away from the path, the grass and the grazing-land, when suddenly the rope tautened between Sinigaglia and Carrel. The rope did not give: up above, Carrel moved no more. He had struggled so far to bring his companions back. Now that they were safe he could die.

'Heartbroken, we cut the rope that tied us to our valiant comrade and continued the descent . . .

'Carrel died like a saint and a hero on his mountain, after having mustered all the energy of which he was capable to save the life of his tourist,' Sinigaglia points out; 'he died after putting his client out of all danger, exhausted by the supreme effort of sixteen hours of unremitting toil in the midst of unending struggles and difficulties, in a blizzard which, in many ways, seemed to be one of those against which there can be no resistance.'

Whymper was to say later: 'Carrel, though always poor, was never greedy of gain. His bold exploits compel our admiration, and the manner of his death rouses our deep sympathy and our respect. The manner of his death strikes a chord in hearts he never knew. He recognized to the fullest extent the duties of his position, and in the closing act of his life set a brilliant example of fidelity and devotion. For it cannot be doubted that, enfeebled as he was, he could have saved himself had he given his attention to self-preservation. He took a nobler course; and, accepting his responsibility, devoted his whole soul to the welfare of his comrades, until utterly exhausted, he fell staggering on the snow.'

The story is told that one day a climber, passing the cross, asked his guide if Carrel had really fallen at that spot. The guide immediately replied, 'No!' For Carrel had not fallen. Carrel had died.

Another Italian, too, loved the Matterhorn in an extraordinary way, thrilling deeply at the mere mention of its name. This man was Guido Rey. He tells how they met for the first time: 'We were drawing near to the bend at the Grands Moulins,' he writes, 'and my companion said to me: "Prepare yourself, in two minutes we shall see the Matterhorn."' That 'Prepare yourself' is wonderful. True, the older man who was initiating the newcomer so well into the mysteries of the heights and the love of the Matterhorn was the son of the founder of the Italian Alpine Club, Guido Rey's uncle, Alexander Sella.

For the young Guido Rey that day was one of revelation. Thenceforward he was often to come to Breuil, not only to see the Matterhorn and climb it, but first and foremost to live in tune with the classic peak, to live side by side with it and breathe the air it breathed.

He was, of course, to climb the Matterhorn several times, by the Lion arête, by the Hörnli arête, by the Zmutt arête, but in the first place he was to be lucky enough to have his house facing that stone cathedral halfway to the sky. Before the climb, there was the experience of making approaches to the mountain in the mind as if to a living being; then came all the spiritual insight gained while making the long ascent. 'It is no fleeting impression that we bring back from up there, but a strong sensation which lasts all our lives,' he writes.

Guido Rey's enduring reputation is due less to his mountaineering career than to his finely poetic and delicately sensitive writings. Nevertheless, his name is also very closely linked with the Furggen arête. In 1890 Guido Rey decided to attack this beautiful ridge, which, from Breuil, is outlined against the sky on the right, and above all to climb the last projection which had repulsed Burgener, Venetz and Mummery. In a week he made three attempts, which is evidence of a great

The tombstone of J.-A. Carrel. Photo: Pierre Tairraz

desire and much perseverance; unfortunately the three attempts failed one after the other, all brought to a halt by bad weather or bad conditions. Guido Rey gave up: 'Reason,' he said, 'prevailed over passion.' For years he tried to forget Furggen, but in vain. 'My friend Vaccarone saw clearly that my soul was a soul in torment,' he writes, 'condemned to wander along the Furggen arête until someone, reaching the summit by that route, managed to disperse the spell.'

Finally Rey could bear it no longer. A new venture was decided upon, and, to try to snatch the victory, it was arranged that a team should come from the top and throw a rope to Rey and his guides, Antoine and Aimé Maquignaz, to enable them to negotiate the overhang. The rendezvous was promptly carried out.

However, climbing a rope swinging below an overhang at a height of 14,200 feet, with an enormous void

Guido Rey. From the collection of Emile Gos.

right-hand page
The topmost part of the Matterhorn, seen from the south-west. On the left: the west face and the Zmutt arête. At first on the right, then in the centre: the Tyndall Peak, the Enjambée and upper part of the Lion arête.
Photo: Bradford Washburn

beneath his feet, after a climb which was already very taxing, was beyond the power of Antoine Maquignaz, even though he was a first-class guide; it was another setback.

Three days later, with wonderful persistence and improved equipment, the team was once again on the spot. The purpose of the expedition was no longer to climb the thirty feet that no one had been able to negotiate, but to explore them. That is why the three men went to the summit this time, came down to the edge of the overhang and fixed a rope ladder attached to a stout piton.

'Antoine went down the ladder,' writes Guido Rey, 'supported by the rope held by his companions; he disappeared for four or five minutes, I don't know exactly; it seemed an eternity to me.'

And when Maquignaz had come up again, it was Guido Rey's turn: 'I grasped the first step of the little ladder and went down. I did not count the number of steps—probably seven or eight. I felt the ladder stretch under my weight and swing from right to left. I placed my foot on a rock foothold without letting go of the ladder: it was the act of taking possession. From above, the guides were now shouting to me to hurry. I climbed back up the little dancing ladder and quickly rejoined them. The ceremony was at an end.'

So the great projection on the Furggen arête was explored; all that remained was to climb it, if possible, directly.

In 1911 Mario Piacenza, Jean-Joseph Carrel and Joseph Gaspard climbed the arête, but turned the great projection on the left.

In 1930, Enzo Benedetti, Louis Carrel and Maurice Bich also went round to the left of the great projection, staying, however closer to the line of the arête.

Finally, in 1941, Louis Carrel, Giacoma Chiara and Alfredo Perino achieved the direct climb of the great overhanging rock.

Louis Carrel is both an exceptional climber and a first-class guide, but first and foremost he is a man of real kindness and great integrity. I have been lucky enough to meet him several times; I attach at least as much importance to the men who climb the mountains as to their successful climbs. The first time I met Louis Carrel was on the Matterhorn, on the lower part of the Hörnli arête. I was at the Hörnli hut when

I heard a guide, who was on his way down from the Matterhorn, say: 'Carrel has just done the traverse, he'll be here soon.' I immediately left with a companion to meet him. We met him halfway between the Hörnli and the Solvay huts. I was happy, and rather moved. What is important between men, whether they are of the same generation or not, is that bond of sympathy which enables them to understand each other without speaking, and which unites them deeply and strongly.

Louis Carrel, often called 'Carrellino', is the man who has contributed most to the modern conquest of the

Louis Carrel on the east face of the Matterhorn.
Photo: Giuseppe Mazzotti

right-hand page
The Weisshorn. Photo: Gaston Rébuffat

pages 174-175
The Dent d'Hérens. Photo: Gaston Rébuffat

Matterhorn; besides his first ascent of the Furggen, he was also the first to climb the south face (and by two different routes) and the east face; moreover, in conditions which progressively worsened as they went higher, under almost uninterrupted stone-falls and despite bad weather which delayed him and his companion to the point of holding them down for many hours on the rock-face, he was probably the first to open up a direct way to the west face. Louis Carrel has achieved success in very great enterprises, and through his personality and his strong and straightforward behaviour he has had an extremely good influence. However, before his vigorous arrival on the scene, a resounding victory in the annals of mountaineering was to take place on the Matterhorn: the first ascent of the north face on 1 August 1931.

Of the four faces of the Matterhorn, the north face is the most severe, the most beautiful and the most awe-inspiring; it is between the Hörnli arête and the Zmutt arête, and is 3,500 feet in height. Seen from the front, from the Zinalrothorn, it has the simplicity of a perfect triangle. Seen from Zermatt, it has the appearance of a gigantic twisted coil of stone. To look at, it seems difficult, but first and foremost it is dangerous. The rock is bad, the ice on it is glassy, there are no halting-places or the slightest protection in case of a storm, but above all there are avalanches of rock and the best techniques are of no avail against them. Only for a few days a year do they refrain from ploughing their way down the rock wall; one has to be there at the right time; but how can one guess it? The Matterhorn is strange and always mysterious.

Since 1923 this great north face, as extraordinary as a symbol, invested with more glory than any other mountain-face, excited the desires of young climbers as enterprising as their elders; the two words 'north face' and 'Matterhorn' were already heavily loaded with significance! Many dreamed of it, yet very few dared to try it: there were no more than three serious attempts. The first was that of the Austrian climbers, Alfred Horeschowsky and Franz Piekelko on 12 August 1923. It created a sensation at the time, and with good reason. From the Hörnli hut the two men crossed to the north face and scaled the ice-slope diagonally with the idea of getting to the great gully which was to serve as a line of ascent for the victors of 1931; but that day

continuous stone-falls denied access to it; they climbed the very steep rocks situated below the Hörnli Shoulder, and after twelve and a half hours of effort, emerged at about 13,000 feet, a few steps away from the Solvay hut on the Hörnli arête.

In September 1928, two guides from Taesch, Victor Imboden and Kaspar Mooser, made an attempt on the opposite side of the face. They thought that in that way they would be less exposed to stone-falls. They climbed thirteen hundred feet in the wide gully which is situated below the great triangle and which falls from the Zmutt arête; then they climbed the rocks that border that gully on its right edge, but above them they came up against insurmountable difficulties, and after twelve hours of continuous effort they were brought to a halt. They bivouacked standing throughout the night, and even before first light, under an ominous sky, they began a descent which was to be carried out almost entirely by abseiling and was to take eleven hours.

On 4 September 1930, Mooser made a fresh attempt, accompanied by M. E. R. Blanchet and Joseph Lärjen. If, in 1928, Mooser had only a reconnaissance in mind, this time he had the clear intention of reaching the summit. However, the team was not to get very high; after having scaled the great ice-slope, they were stopped by verglas which covered all the rocks.

The following year, at the beginning of August, the incredible news went around the streets of Zermatt and spread from one end of the Alps to the other; the north face of the Matterhorn had just been climbed!

Anderl Heckmair, the future victor of the north face of the Eiger, was at the Torino hut when he heard it; among young German climbers the 'great problems' were the order of the day—the north faces of the Matterhorn, the Grandes Jorasses, the Eiger—and Heckmair was not surprised by the success. However, he was expecting others to be the conquerors: 'We were already rejoicing at the victory of our friends Léo Rittler and Hans Brehm (who were to be killed a few days later on the north face of the Grandes Jorasses)

when we learned that victory had in fact been won by Toni and Franz Schmid. Although we count these two brothers also among our good friends, they had maintained absolute secrecy, and we knew nothing of their intentions.'

In mid-July the two young Germans had left Munich on bicycles. Franz, the elder, in fact, only wanted to make a few good climbs, but Toni, younger and bolder, stood his ground and had his way—the north face of the Matterhorn!

Half an hour before midnight, when they had hardly fallen asleep, they were awake again and on their feet. They left their tent and reached the foot of the north face in silence. 'Before us, appallingly steep, rose the ice slope, about 1,000 feet high, which, we thought, should enable us to negotiate the lower part of the wall. Towards the top it was lost in the blackness of sheer rocks. By way of the steep avalanche-cone, we reached the yawning bergschrund. It was three forty-five, and still dark.'

At last, at four o'clock, Toni started upon the ice-slope, with Franz following. 'Relying only on our crampons, there we were, the two of us, on the sheer wall,' writes Toni.

For long hours, all day, almost without a pause, they climbed the icy rocks. 'It was a desperate struggle with the mountain. Foot by foot we advanced. Our fingers, scraped raw, were bleeding. What did that matter! Onwards towards the summit! We had to get away from that fearful wall! Rocks of all sizes went humming past our ears and fell into the depths. We paid no attention to them.'

The sun was now low. 'We continued to advance painfully,' writes Toni Schmid. 'The ropes, stiff with frost, became difficult to handle. Another hour slipped away in superhuman efforts, but progress was slower and slower. With ever greater difficulty, I still pressed on. The obstacles hardly varied, but our strength was diminishing.'

At last, at half past eight, they reached a place to spend the night. They fixed two pitons, to which they tied themselves, and slipped into their sleeping bags. 'Our sole preoccupation,' writes Toni, 'was not to lose our balance. We almost had the feeling of floating in space, detached from the earth.'

It was so cold that they did not leave the bivouac

The Dent Blanche.
Photo: Gaston Rébuffat

until seven o'clock. Toni set off in the lead, then his brother took over from him, but ice-covered slabs barred his way. 'With clenched teeth, Franz advanced another yard,' writes Toni. 'With hasty axe-strokes he tried to clear the rock of its coating of ice. In vain! It was impossible to get past that cursed slab. He came down again to the place where he had been shortly before. His courage seemed about to forsake him.

'"We shan't get any further!" he shouted to me. "We'll have to try to get to the Swiss arête!" "What! Give up so near the goal?" I said. "Try to traverse to the right. It seems to me there's a chance of getting through there."'

Franz regained confidence. 'Cautiously he traversed to the right and cut steps in the thin ice. Would it hold? What would happen if it gave way? We had not the time to imagine it. We had to go forward. It was ahead that safety lay. A distant roll of thunder forced us to hurry. The weather, so fine a short while ago, had worsened little by little, and cold mists were now rending themselves on the wall and the arêtes. The energy of despair helped us to get over the bad patch.' At last 'something dark emerged from the mist. Was it the summit? With palpitating heart, we quickened our pace, only to return soon to our monotonous rhythm: it was not the summit!'

The two brothers were resuming the climb when, suddenly and violently, the storm burst. 'The wind, which had become a hurricane, drove sheets of hail before it. In a moment the steps we cut were filled in. We struggled on beneath the waves of the storm, abandoned to its fury. The lightning flashes were hurled down, the air was saturated with electricity, and our ice-axes whistled ominously. But nothing would stop us from advancing.'

At two o'clock in the afternoon, in the middle of the storm, Toni and Franz Schmid at last reached the summit. 'What did the unfettered elements matter from then onwards! We ran along the arête to hide our ice-axes near the iron cross, and a few feet lower down we found shelter under an overhang at the moment when

Franz and Toni Schmid, victors of the north face of the Matterhorn. From the collection of Emile Gos

the storm reached its climax. There beneath the protection of our groundsheet, our hands met in a silent grasp. We tried to assuage our stomach pangs with a little chocolate. We could hardly believe that we had escaped from the fearful wall where we had had virtually superhuman difficulties to struggle against. From the furious and continuous howling one would have said that the mountain was not resigned to its defeat. Showers of light set the arête afire, and the terrible explosions of the thunder prevented our feeling of triumph from really flowering.'

They took advantage of a slight lull to begin the descent by way of the Hörnli arête. A second storm, more terrible than the first, took them by surprise at the Shoulder. 'Snow and hail rushed in torrents to the foot of the rocks. In the twinkling of an eye a thick coating of ice covered the rope. In this state it was more of a handicap than a help. Our clothes were squeezing us like armour when, at five-thirty in the evening, we at last reached the Solvay hut.'

With much difficulty they untied the frozen rope; they put their clothes in a corner of the hut, wrapped themselves in all the blankets, swallowed the rest of their provisions and fell into a deep sleep.

The next day they did not wake up until noon. The storm continued. They tried to appease their hunger with maize and old crusts of bread which they found in the hut. Then they fell asleep again.

On the morning of August 3rd, the sun woke them. The storm was over. At seven o'clock they left the hut. At half past twelve they were with their friends who had come to meet them.

That evening Zermatt gave them a triumphal reception. 'We were overcome with the delicious sensation of victory and only then did we realize the magnitude of the problem we had just solved.'

Indeed, the first ascent of the north face of the Matterhorn was a great date in the history of that celebrated mountain; moreover, it was to be the starting signal for the ascents of the other faces, and, going far beyond even the confines of Matterhorn history, it marked the beginning of a 're-conquest' of all the peaks by way of their most difficult faces. The impetus had been given by a spectacular success on the most beautiful and awe-inspiring of the faces, and on the Matterhorn the reply was to come without delay: two and a half months later, on 15 October 1931, the Italians achieved the first ascent of the wild and very vast south face. True, they had been dreaming of it for a long time, and as with the 'Bersagliere' seventy years earlier, a profound emotion was mingled with their desire for conquest: the south face was not merely a mountain wall to be climbed—it was an extension of their valley leading towards the sky. Whymper on one hand, and the Schmid brothers on the other, had one aim: to reach a summit, to scale a face. No question of love was involved—and that was normal.

The Italians' desire, however, was paired with an affectionate, almost filial feeling—a well-known characteristic of the people of the Val d'Aosta. It is only fair to acknowledge that, unlike the men of Zermatt, who were present at the conquest of the summit, the faces and the arêtes without ever actually taking the initiative, the inhabitants of Valtournanche were not content just to take part in the successes of others, but themselves played a decisive role.

Amilcar Crétier was one of those young men from the Val d'Aosta for whom the mountain was everything. Whenever he had a moment to spare, Crétier climbed a peak, even if it was not an important peak. Yet it was the Matterhorn that attracted him most, and, curiously enough, although he was to achieve more than fifty 'firsts' in the Mont Blanc, Grivola and Grand Paradis massifs, he was to have no luck on the Matterhorn.

At Christmas he came to study the south face. In summer he made an attempt alone, and climbed to 13,000 feet below the Furggen Shoulder. His companion Binel arrived later, but with him came bad weather.

Enzo Benedetti, who had climbed the Furggen arête the year before, and from there had examined the possibilities of climbing the south face, was also in Breuil; however, rain and snow prevented his making any attempt. Now the summer was over, and the larches had assumed the beautiful tint of autumn, when suddenly Benedetti received a telegram telling him to come. He hurried there, met Louis Carrel and Maurice Bich, and the same evening the three men slept at l'Oriondé. The following day, October 15th, at five in the morning, they set out; the weather was fine, it was wonderful, they were alone on the mountain.

They traversed eastwards so as to reach a point vertically below the summit, then they climbed rapidly. They were filled with joy. In their enthusiasm, instead of reaching the summit by a slight diversion to the left, as they had planned, they mounted directly, with Carrel in the lead, by the central gully, 'where even a cat would not climb' and so, without detour, succeeded brilliantly in the first ascent of the south face.

A winter went by, and other plans matured. On 16 September 1932, six climbers coming from Breuil arrived at the Hörnli hut: Enzo Benedetti with the guides Louis Carrel and Maurice Bich, who were on the south face, and three friends, Giuseppe Mazzotti and the guides Lucien Carrel and Antoine Gaspard; they intended to climb the east face. The difficulty would be the scaling of the final steep rock, and the initial danger lay in reaching it by climbing the first three-quarters of the face, exposed as it was, in view of its orientation, to stone-falls from the moment the sun appeared.

In complete darkness, despite an alarm-clock which had failed to ring, they left the hut, crossed the glacier, reached the foot of the face, and by the time the sunlight came to warm them, they were already at a good height. Maurice Bich had been struck on the head by a stone, but not seriously hurt. They made all the haste they could up the steady slope, passed the level of the Shoulder, and without any detour, reached directly the great ascending ledge which, from the Furggen arête, obliquely cuts the 'head' of the Matterhorn and comes out on the Hörnli arête. Mist took possession of the wall. They could have used this ledge to escape towards the right, but Carrel went slightly off towards the left, over a slab of red rock, in order to get to the centre of the face, directly below the summit. From then onwards their difficulties were extreme. Night fell before they could reach the summit, and they had to bivouac on the rock-face itself, in difficult conditions.

The next day the six men climbed the last 130 feet,

and at eight-thirty all six were together, side by side, on the summit, having climbed up that steep part, which is relatively short but extremely difficult, and without any level places—a feat which had been regarded as impossible, even with a bivouac.

Thus five direct routes had been traced out on the north, south and east faces. On the south face, vast as it is, there even existed a secondary route, climbing along the south spur of Tyndall Peak. Ugo de Amicis and Arrigo Frusta had opened it up in 1906, but at the level of the Cravate, being unable to climb the top of the spur, they had traversed to the right to get to the Lion arête. In 1933, Amilcar Crétier, Antoine Gaspard and Basile Ollietti straightened this route by forcing their way up the top part of the climb and reaching Tyndall Peak directly; unhappily, descending by way of the Lion arête, they fell between the 'Linceul' and the 'Grande Tour' and were killed.

In 1941 Albert Deffeyes and Louis Carrel, accompanied by Pierre Maquignaz, achieved a 'first' of a quite special kind— the circuit of the 'Tête du Cervin'! By way of the Swiss arête they climbed to the Hörnli Shoulder, and from there they traversed successively the east face, the south face, the west face and the north face, at a height of between 13,000 and 14,000 feet, returned to the Hörnli Shoulder, and from there reached the summit. If it had come from anyone but Carrel, this would have seemed ridiculous; to him it was just another way of thoroughly covering his mountain, not to mention the fact that in that way he would, if the need arose, have a very exact appreciation of the 'feel' of each of the four faces.

The following year Louis Carrel and Albert Deffeyes achieved another 'first' of the most perilous kind on the south face: they climbed the long rib that rises parallel to the Amicis arête in a straight line from the Matterhorn glacier to Tyndall Peak close by the Enjambée.

So the Matterhorn was explored on all its sides. However, one face remained relatively unexplored. Penhall had partially used the west side, but the problem of that face had not been solved.

After the adventure of Lammer and Lorria, this great face which dominates the Tiefenmatten Glacier was, in 1929, the setting for another, and no less remarkable, exploit. On July 18th, without a companion—he had

waited for him in vain in Zermatt—and without crampons (which he had forgotten), a young Viennese climber, Fritz Hermann, arrived at the foot of the Penhall couloir. Faced with this double handicap, most climbers would doubtless have given up, but Hermann carried on, and, a lonely, tiny human presence on the immense rock wall, he climbed by following, more or less, Penhall's route. He did not stop until nightfall, and bivouacked on a level surface 'as wide as a rucksack', surrounded by mist and flashes of lightning. The next day, in the sun, which had reappeared, he reached the summit, then descended to Zermatt by way of the Hörnli arête.

In 1931 Amilcar Crétier and Léonard Pession came to the foot of the west face that they had so often contemplated from the Italian arête. Their aim was to open up a new route, but the route they covered was to be more in the nature of an escapade than a real itinerary. In fact, they climbed the lower part of the Penhall couloir; then instead of heading for the summit, they undertook a long traverse which, two days later, brought them to a height of 12,000 feet on the Italian arête. Bad weather had been with them almost from the beginning. Conditions were unfavourable, the long traverse was carried out with the almost continuous threat of stone-falls, and came to nothing. They arrived at a nondescript point on the Lion arête. But it mattered little; Crétier's and Pession's underlying aim was to live through hours of intense experience in intimate contact with the rock face: their wish was realized to the full.

However, the route up the west face still remained to be opened up: a route which would go straight from the glacier to the summit, without detour, without flinching; not a hybrid route using first the face and then the Zmutt arête, but one which would negotiate the upper steep part, not go round it; climbing, as it were, the trajectory of a stone falling from the summit directly on to the frozen solitudes of Tiefenmatten.

Louis Carrel, of course, had been dreaming of it for a long time; he decided to set out on 19 August 1947; Carlo Taddei was with him. From Breuil they crossed the Col Tournanche to reach the foot of the wall. They had certainly expected stone-falls, but they were amazed and terrified by their volume.

For two days they were to play a wretched game of

hide-and-seek with them; sometimes they remained imprisoned beneath a shelter for hours; then, taking advantage of a lull, they would climb with the greatest difficulty over rock that was now safe, now friable, a small part of the time in fine weather, but much of it under snow. Conditions were so bad, the climbing so hard, and the dangers so continuous that during the second day they gained only five hundred feet in height. In view of Carrel's experience, his technical skill, mountaineering sense and sheer ability, one can imagine what it was like! On the morning after the third bivouac the weather was still bad. The stone-falls had lessened, but there were now avalanches of snow instead, which were no better. The guide and his young companion at last managed to get off the rock face; they came on to the Italian arête at the level of the Enjambée.

Carrel's exploit was extraordinary, but above all one must admire his honesty. Without beating about the bush, he writes: 'A new route has been opened up on the Matterhorn, but the western wall still remains inviolate.'

Fifteen years later, on 13 August 1962, two men from the Val d'Aosta, René Daguin and Jean Ottin, successfully climbed the direct route at last: they virtually followed Penhall's route as long as it stayed on the west face, and where it diverged from it at the level of the central névé to approach the Zmutt arête, Daguin and Ottin veered away in the other direction, to the right, to climb by way of a couloir which led them to Carrel's Corridor, at the foot of the final triangular pitch. 'Above us, the unknown,' writes Ottin. Suddenly, things became very difficult, or rather, extremely delicate: it was all a question of balance. With the help of pitons, Ottin nevertheless managed to continue the climb; at half past two in the afternoon Ottin and Daguin reached the top: the west face had surrendered its last secrets.

WINTER ASCENTS

And yet, is it not in the nature of man to love a challenge and always to seek out difficulties?

That is why another campaign of conquest, begun on 18 March 1882, by Vittorio Sella, Jean-Antoine and Louis Carrel, when they made the first winter ascent of the Matterhorn, was to be continued and intensified.

Winter renewed the mystery. The cold, the distance, the separation, the covering of snow, the short days, all re-created the original conditions. Having at their disposal on the one hand the experience of the early climbers, and, on the other, constantly improved technique and equipment, it was logical that younger generations, having no longer a virgin wall to conquer, should turn to winter ascents.

In March 1948, the Zmutt arête was climbed by M. Masson and the guide Edmund Petrig, and in March 1952, Roberto Bignami and Walter Bonatti made the first winter ascent of the whole Furggen arête; that is to say, by scaling the great step directly.

In 1961 it was the north face which was the object of winter attempts. Walter Bonatti tried in March, and Hilti von Allmen and Paul Etter in December, nine months later. Christmas went by, and the new year came: at the beginning of January, from 7th to the 9th, Hiebeler, Kinshofer, Krempke and Mazeaud tried in their turn. On January 23rd the Austrians Adolf and Franz Huber and Hubert Seldmayer failed narrowly; they had climbed the most difficult sections, but at 13,800 feet a storm was raging. They gave up their attempt on the summit, traversed towards the Hörnli arête and reached the Solvay hut.

Finally a few days later, on February 3rd, the once-for-all assault was made. Seven men tried their luck, as on 14 July 1865, almost a century before, but divided into three independent teams. Despite the storm, which was to take them by surprise, they were to succeed magnificently, without accident. 'In view of the fact that Paul Etter and I envisaged a rapid rate of ascent,' writes Hilti von Allmen, 'they let us start out ahead.' In the second position came the other two-man rope, the Austrians Leo Schlömmer and Erich Krempke. And last of all was the three-man team, less fast by definition, and composed of the Germans Werner Bittner, Peter Siegert and Rainer Kauschke. 'In spite of our friendly rivalry,' continues von Allmen, 'all seven of us had decided to back up and support one another in case of necessity.' So it was almost a 'collective' that, at five o'clock in the morning, reached the foot of the famous rock-face and began to climb the slope. The thermometer was showing $-25°C$;

however, everyone was carefully equipped: von Allmen and Etter had each brought three pairs of gloves, among other things; they also had a tiny transistor radio, with a view to getting news of the weather. At eight o'clock they reached the top of the ice slope, at 12,000 feet. From the start, each pitch was climbed using pitons, and so it continued right to the summit. The climbers reached the great couloir. 'Up to this point we had left our pitons in place for our companions. But from the beginning of the dièdre, because of the considerable lead we had taken, we were compelled to retrieve our pitons. If we had left them in position we would have been obliged to wait, which was contrary to our common agreement and our personal plan—or we would have been short of pitons. At noon the great dièdre which rises towards the Zmutt arête was at our feet. The altimeter showed 12,800 feet.'

Higher up, they were to climb the steepest and most difficult pitch of the route, and that took a great deal of time. 'I noticed that it was five o'clock,' writes von Allmen. 'So we concentrated on finding an acceptable bivouac site.'

'Here, at any rate, we shall be able to sit down,' shouted Etter, who was leading. Von Allmen went to join him, but as he moved, his crampons, which he had taken off for the moment because his feet were too cold, slid away down the slope.

At 13,300 feet the two guides prepared their bivouac, while the Austrians and the Germans stopped lower down. At seven in the evening von Allmen set off a green rocket as a signal that all was well. Then he listened to his transistor radio: the weather forecast for the following day was not good. 'The lights of Zermatt, far away beneath my feet,' writes von Allmen, 'seemed to belong to another world . . . The time passed with infinite slowness, but morning came after

The Matterhorn: facing, the north wall, between the Zmutt arête to the right and the Hörnli arête to the left; extreme left, the Furggen arête, and in front of it the east face. Drawing by Bichet

pages 188-189
'Tête du Cervin': in profile on the left, the Furggen arête, facing, on the left, the Hörnli arête; on the right, the Zmutt arête; between the Hörnli arête and the Zmutt arête, the north wall. Photo: Bradford Washburn

BICHET

all, and at nine o'clock on Sunday, February 4th, we were on the move again.'

Towards half past one in the afternoon, as they were emerging from great difficulties, they saw the Austrians and Germans reaching the level of their bivouac. The weather turned stormy, snow fell, and mist enveloped them. Fortunately they were not far from the summit. At three-thirty Etter reached the cross, and Allmen joined him. 'We shook hands in silence, then took the inevitable photo. A real hurricane was blowing there in squalls. This made it twice as cold. Only then did I notice that my fingers were hard and numb. This was the result of losing my crampons: I had had to cling too often to the snow and ice.'

Without delay they descended by way of the Hörnli arête, but the storm was so violent that they could not get to the Solvay hut. They bivouacked 260 feet above it, in a hollow they dug in the snow.

The next day they took an hour to descend those 260 feet, and at 9.30 they reached the hut. 'We discovered no trace of our comrades there. During the day the blizzard continued to rage with steady violence. We shouted into the storm until we lost our voices, but there was no reply. We could do nothing but wait, hope and . . . pray that the five men would nevertheless find the strength to reach us.

'Meanwhile, evening came. Paul stood in front of the hut for the last time and shouted with all the strength of his lungs. Then came a barely audible reply, faint at first, but growing louder: yes, it was they; so we were all safe. All five of them arrived at 7.30, and told us, to our great joy, that they too had reached the summit in the afternoon of that February 5th.'

The next evening, February 6th, the seven climbers arrived at Zermatt, where a magnificent reception awaited them. They took pleasure in the congratulations and the honours, yet Hilti von Allmen, a guide at Lauterbrunnen, concludes, 'In our heart of hearts we still feel that the mountains will always be greater than the men who climb them.'

Finally, in 1965, between February 18th and 22nd, Walter Bonatti accomplished a very great feat: alone, in winter, he made a successful ascent of the north face of the Matterhorn, and, into the bargain, traced a new way up it, to the right of the Schmid brothers' route.

First he climbed the slopes used by Kaspar Mooser and Victor Imboden in their 1928 attempt; with great difficulty, and with the help of pitons, he succeeded in negotiating the overhanging 'dorsal' which had halted the two Valais guides.

Being alone, he had to cover each difficult stretch three times: 'This is how I advanced,' writes Bonatti: 'I fixed my rucksack to a piton, then I climbed the length of the rope, tied the other end of the rope to another piton, came down again to get the rucksack, then went up once more, taking out the pitons as I went along.'

Each bivouac was a worse ordeal than the last. At times he became somewhat disheartened, but on each occasion he recovered his spirits admirably, and finally, on February 22nd, he reached the summit.

The papers seized upon the news avidly: *Epoca* and *Match* subsequently published Bonatti's story.

'At about three in the afternoon, at barely two hundred feet from the summit, the cross appeared to me,' wrote Bonatti. 'In the sun which illumined it, it seemed incandescent. The light which emanated from it dazzled me. It was a supernatural, miraculous thing, like the haloes of the saints. The planes which up to that point had deafened me with the noise of their engines seemed to guess that something had happened. As if from a feeling of modesty, they flew away and left me alone.

'Then, as if hypnotized, I stretched out my arms towards the cross until I could feel its metal substance right against my chest. And I fell to my knees and wept in silence.'

THE MATTERHORN—
THE MOUNTAIN AND THE DREAM

THE NORTH FACE

How many years did I, like so many others, have to wait before seeing and climbing it!

Years of revelations, of inner discoveries and passionate approaches; bent over books and maps, pictures and photographs, I read, I looked, and very soon I was no longer just an enthusiastic spectator: I already belonged to the enchanted peak.

Years of waiting which were not time lost, for it is due to them that the mountains seem so beautiful.

We are thought to be mind-wandering, but we are devotees. We are riding at anchor, waiting to set forth; we have not yet started, but we are already in motion: long before one has roped up, the climb has begun. Throughout the long winters and summers a man shapes, constructs, creates his mountain. The great longings are composed of virility and a little melancholy. And then we have to find the companion whose heart beats in time with our own, for without this, for me at least, the climb loses some of its quality. I admire solitary climbers, and I understand their exclusive passion, but that is not my way.

During the climb, and even on the summit, we hardly speak, but the rope, a material bond, and much more than that, is between us. For a guide, a summit is far more beautiful when he sees the joy of it in his companions' eyes.

I like climbing in autumn; the air is crisper, the colours purer. How many times have I climbed thalwegs which have regained their silence, and which the darkness and the cold already have in their grip. The hoar-frost covers them but up above, one comes into a landscape of light; the distant campanile of Val Montanaia, the wild Drus, the Innominata on Mont Blanc, the south arête of the Noire, and many others more often climbed in season and even when the season is well past; the last visit, then nostalgia. Then comes a time of fruitful anticipation.

Occasionally, to allay impatience, there is a winter climb; the rocks are covered with ice, fingers are cold; the climb is quite an accomplishment, but it has a different sort of charm.

Then comes the opening of the season: our blood seethes, the call becomes irresistible.

It was in these last days of June that I first went to Zermatt and the Valais to see, and then climb the Matterhorn. The year was 1949, and I had been climbing for eleven years—eleven years during which, after seeing the Matterhorn in books, I had caught sight of it, glimpsed it, guessed at it from the Dauphiné, the Mont Blanc massif or the Oberland.

The little train climbed slowly, engaged the rack and pinion, disengaged it, stopped at the stations; the landscape was beautiful, nature was being born again, the countryside was smiling, but that day there was something stronger in me that could not be appeased with beautiful picture postcards. To be precise, the great plan had been in my mind since autumn: to climb the north face of the Matterhorn.

191

By my side was my companion. He climbed well, but he was not merely a good climber; he belonged to the mountains; he was a kinsman of the snow, the wind and the stars. For the Matterhorn that is doubly important—for the ascent itself and its technical aspect, but also in order that our hearts should be in tune with the mountain we were going to climb. Raymond Simond loved climbing, but he also loved just to be among the mountains. He had climbed the Spigolo Giallo, he loved the smell of the rock; he also loved the fragrance of the forest in which he lived; and he loved the silence and the murmerings of nature. He often looked at the sky, for no reason but the sheer pleasure of it.

And now, while the little train jolted us along with its anonymous crowd, the moment was approaching when we would see the Matterhorn!

One is always afraid of being disappointed. If one's dreams should not come true . . . if it was not quite what one had imagined . . . exactitude and truth are often quite different things!

The truth is the ideal peak, alone, unique, classic. The truth is 1860, the look in the eyes of Carrel and Whymper, the years of waiting, Croz and his straightforwardness; it is 1865, the victory and the catastrophe, the enthusiasm and the self-denial of the Abbé Gorret, it is Penhall, Mummery, Guido Rey, Crétier, Carrellino, Mazzotti, the Schmid brothers who set out from home on bicycles; it is also the countless climbers who have reached the summit since the first ascent, it is also the loyalty of Edward Monod-Herzen, who, at seventy-nine, returned to the Matterhorn for the thirteenth time. The truth is the Matterhorn and so much love in the hearts of men!

Whymper consumed with impatience.

Whymper, Carrel and the others . . . .

We were their heirs.

At one o'clock in the morning, on June 27th, we moved silently along the base of the séracs that protect the north face. We had descended too far, but, finding a way through, we insinuated ourselves between the huge blocks of ice and reached the upper plateau. It was very cold—a good sign. We were alone; there was no one even on the arête at the beginning of the season.

At first light we crossed the bergschrund. The bergschrund is a break which marks a change in the gradient of the slope; it also marked a break in our frame of mind: we left the gentle lines of approach to reach abruptly the sheer lines of the rock wall; we passed from easy walking to severe climbing: crossing the bergschrund is to cross the frontier between two worlds. At first we climbed together, very quickly, using crampons on the steep slope. The snow was as hard as one could wish, but higher up it became horrible—powdery, light, giving way on a base of solid ice. We had come at the beginning of the season so that there would be no stone-falls, and so as to be alone; we would be safe, but, on the other hand, the mountain was in bad condition: on this terribly cold north face the snow had not yet stabilized. We had to cut steps, that, too, was part of our job, and a not unpleasing one; cutting a step with the minimum number of axe-strokes is an art in itself. Before the point where the slope butted up against the rocks, we traversed to the right to get to the couloir, the key section of the middle third of the climb, and the most difficult part of this north face. However, we only traversed it: it seemed too dangerous to us. We were going to try to climb the wall to the right which separates the couloir from the Zmutt arête, a very steep wall, more difficult than the couloir, but also less dangerous. In mountain-climbing there is an intimate, secret pleasure in guessing, sensing things in advance. Shortly after we had crossed this couloir, an avalanche of stones—we could hardly see it, but we heard it clearly—hurtled to the bottom of the couloir, from which rose a cloud of snow-dust and a smell of shattered rocks.

The wall is not vertical, like a limestone face, but the climb is just as exposed, without a single level surface. Oh, the eternal promise of a little ledge which retreats as one climbs towards it! On that vast north face there are no well-defined pitches; everything looks the same; there are no geometrical figures as on the walls of the Mont Blanc range. Except for a few major lines—the Zmutt arête on the extreme right, the couloir to the left and the Shoulder above, there are no landmarks. We could not say: 'We have just climbed the Grade V crack, or the 250-foot dièdre.' There is no 'Grade V

The top of the ice slope on the north face of the Matterhorn. Photo: Gaston Rébuffat

crack' to find and climb; there is no '250-foot dièdre', no characteristic slab, no second- or sixth-grade chimney. No. We simply climbed as well as the terrain allowed, on that immense inclined plane. We did not have the satisfaction of coming to the end of a very difficult pitch which marks a stage in an ascent, like the Tour Grise on the Grandes Jorasses, or the barrier of roofs on the Piz Badile. We did an undistinguished, patient job. But we were captivated by a strange, slightly crazy charm, by the vertigo of being drowned in a mass of frozen stones. The game was to enter, of one's own free will, the prison which is the north wall of the Matterhorn, and then to escape from it. And the interest lay in finding the safest way out.

There is nowhere to belay on those steep, crumbling slabs, held by the frost, shining with verglas, linked together by patches of black ice under the beautiful disguise of powdery snow. We did not use pitons: they were too hard or too easy to drive in, and they had little hold. At the very most I fixed two during a traverse; Raymond pulled them out with his fingers. From time to time the beautiful pyramid crumbled a little: avalanches of stones fell, whistling. Seen from a distance, the Matterhorn looks unbreakable in its pyramidal soberness and rigidity. It seems as though the winds sharpen it rather than wear or rock it. But when climbing it, one cannot understand how this heap of stones soldered together by ice can have so much vital grace. Nothing holds firm. Immense flakes of rock sit one on top of another like giddy piles of plates. Everything is as if suspended, and life itself seems a temporary reprieve.

And yet, what sacrilege to imagine a Matterhorn truncated, worn, rounded like the mountains round about! No, when climbing this enchanted peak, this fragment of the earth pointing towards the sky, one willingly endows these stones with a magical vigour: they will never grow old; the mountain will stand for ever, and remain the symbol of earth's aspiration towards heaven.

On this north face there are no colours, only a uniform tint which has the reflection of the ice. We climbed with crampons, and we were to keep them on throughout the climb, because there was a great deal of snow on the face. The struggle, though never extreme, was unremitting throughout. Not a quarter of an hour of respite, not five minutes, not one instant: nothing but glassy slabs, gullys and patches of black ice coated with immaculate snow, and always flakes of rock balanced one on top of another. And oh, the wonderful force of gravity! We could never pull on a hand-hold for fear it would come away like an opening drawer and threaten the balance of the entire structure. Earlier on Raymond had broken one of the front spikes of his left crampon, but that did not prevent him from carrying on, as sure-footed as ever. An ideal companion, always cheerful, always at ease on this never very difficult but continuously delicate, high-mountain terrain, a patchwork of ice and rock.

The final slopes were less steep; we were now at 14,000 feet, 650 feet below the summit. The hours had passed, arduous and happy; soon it would be the end of the day, and for us the end of the climb. We gained this impression from a multitude of signs we knew well, and that, familiar and agreeable, we always meet each time we approach a summit. One emerges as if from a pit, and everything around becomes lighter, more airy. This applies both to things and sensations: the taste of the air is drier, the mass of rock and snow shrinks to give place to the sky. On the Matterhorn this impression is extraordinarily vivid. As we rose higher, the two arêtes, Zmutt on the right and Hörnli on the left, had closed in around us. In view of the geometrical purity of the Matterhorn, its pyramidal shape, the triangular form of its walls and the regularity of the slope of the north face, the drawing closer of the Zmutt and Hörnli arêtes, and their need to feel themselves side by side at the moment of attaining the infinite azure, give an impression that is beautiful in its intensity. We were

left-hand page
Looking down on to the top of the ice-slope and the rocks which dominate it. Photo: Gaston Rébuffat

pages 196 and 197
After crossing the couloir. Photo: Gaston Rébuffat.
Traverse towards the centre of the wall.
Photo: Gaston Rébuffat

pages 198 and 199
Midway up the wall. Photo: Gaston Rébuffat.
The top part of the wall. Photo: Gaston Rébuffat

climbing along the bisecting line, and we were about to reach the summit, while behind us, we felt it in our innermost being, without any need to look—the slope of the north face fell away, widening between the two arêtes, which receded and diverged, to anchor themselves, one to the north-west, the other to the north-east, and to hold between them, well tautened and barely concave, the great sheet of frozen rocks which was our wall.

At nine in the evening we reached the summit-ridge. At our altitude the sun, for the Matterhorn and for us, was shedding its last rays. Below, darkness had possessed the valleys; a trail of light indicated the street of Zermatt; on the other side, over Breuil, a little stardust lighted, uncertainly as yet, a few houses and chalets. It was late, and, although we were in June, darkness was not far off. Beneath our feet the great slope fell away. The north face. A disagreeable climb, a wonderful ascent!

Frail men, on the summit of the mountain that points towards the sky. We were there when the earth was put to bed; then, with the earth, we drowsed off in the darkness.

FURGGEN AND THE STORM

Four years later, Paul Beylier, Paul Habran and I left Courmayeur for Breuil, which we had never visited before. I do not normally like three-man ropes, at any rate on rock climbs, for reasons not only of safety, but also of pleasure. I feel I must sense the living presence of my companion through the rope. Now, if, after the second man, there is a third, it is obvious that he is not attached directly to the leader. That day, however, all three of us were very happy to be together. My two companions were excellent mountaineers. Paul Beylier had had a great deal of experience; he had been climbing for twenty years and had ascended all the peaks of his native Dauphiné, often by the hardest routes, and many summits of the Mont Blanc range. Paul Habran had come to the Alps more recently, but he was very gifted, and the previous year, within ten days, we had climbed together the north face of the Grandes Jorasses by way of the Walker Spur, and Mont Maudit by the Tour Ronde arête, to return from Courmayeur to Chamonix and the north face of the Eiger.

We sensed that in those next few days our appetite for the mountains was to be abundantly satisfied. We were going to see the Matterhorn from the Italian side and climb it by way of the Furggen arête for the first time. Having left Courmayeur too late, we were unable, despite a mad rush, to reach Breuil in time to catch the evening cable-railway and spend the night at the Furggenjoch. Compelled to stay in the valley, we wandered about in Cervinia, that new, soulless village that has smothered Breuil and entirely ignores its cathedral.

In vain we looked for a sign, a reminder. Veiled that evening in a cloak of clouds puffed out like a crinoline, the legendary Matterhorn was, however, discreetly alive. We waited for the favourable breeze that would uncover it. We talked of nothing but the mountain and those who had loved it. Were we not in the valley of the Carrels?

When on the following morning the first cable-car put us down at the Furggenjoch, it was already nine o'clock, yet the sea of clouds still filled the Italian valleys as far as the eye could see. In the presence of this extraordinary spectacle we forgot for a while that we had also come to climb.

Taking up our rucksacks again, we followed the easy crest that leads from the cableway to the foot of the Furggen arête. We reached it at half past ten. We were hungry, but I suspect, too, that we wanted to watch the interplay of the clouds, as they rolled and evaporated. In any case, we had to have breakfast, so we decided we might as well have it here, where there was a little stream.

At about eleven o'clock we began the climb. The first 1,500 feet were not difficult; we had to use the east face. We climbed together, merry as students out for a walk. There was a freshness in our hearts, as in our early days as mountaineers.

At 12,000 feet the slope became steeper, and the snow, melting freely at this late hour, was trickling down in abundance. Shortly afterwards we reached the Shoulder at the foot of the great Furggen projection.

right-hand page
The top of the Hörnli arête. Photo: Gaston Rébuffat
pages 202-203
The summit of the Matterhorn. Photo: Gaston Rébuffat

With great care we carried out an awe-inspiring traverse to the left: in this way we passed from the moderate slope of the east face on to a ledge as aerial as the gondola of a balloon, dominating about 3,000 feet of the south face.

For a moment I searched for the way, and took time to choose the best path. We had to traverse another 200 feet or so to follow the Piacenza route that we had decided, the day before, to climb. However, my companions, with one accord, said smilingly: 'Look, straight up above you there's a first piton, and ten feet above that there's a second with a stirrup.'

I had seen them, of course, but we had not set out to attempt Louis Carrel's extremely difficult direct way, marked out by those two pitons. I had not brought the equipment for that ascent, and, after those hours of calm contemplation followed by an easy climb on the east face, I was not tempted by a highly acrobatic pitch that would demand all my concentration; and that empty space, suddenly yawning behind me on the south face, filled me with awe. In the Dolomites, along sheer and sometimes overhanging walls as on the Cima Grande or the Spigolo Giallo, empty space below one is inevitable after the first few feet; here, on the other hand, after comfortable slopes, we were suddenly thrust straight into the sky.

Was it the feeling for the aesthetic, elegant, direct route that impelled me? Habran was already getting into position to belay me and help me to climb on to Beylier, who was giving me a shoulder. Then, inviting me to 'take off', Habran pointed out to me holds that my blind fingers could not find. At last I reached the first piton, then the second. It moved me deeply to cling to these bits of iron, fixed by Louis Carrel, worthy successor to the great Jean-Antoine. I said to myself: 'If the pioneer could have seen the young guide perched on the stirrups to complete the conquest, what happiness would have been his, without a doubt!' Maybe that sums up the history of alpinism.

left-hand page
Descent from the Italian summit. Photo: Pierre Tairraz
page 206
The 'Crête du Coq' on the Lion arête. Photo: Pierre Tairraz
page 207
The Luigi Amedeo hut and the Grande Tour on the Lion arête. Photo: Pierre Tairraz

Above, the crumbling and yet vertical rock—that rock that constitutes the miracle of the Matterhorn, the proud mountain, the rock that is not a joy to climb like the honest granite of the Grépon or the Aiguilles du Diable, that sad, difficult rock forsaken by the sun—was not to my taste, and I wanted to get back to my companions and resume the previous day's plan, the much less difficult Piacenza route. But getting back was more easily said than done. It is far trickier to descend than to climb, and in this particular spot it was absolutely impossible. If I had tried it I would have stood a good chance of falling.

There was, then, no choice; I had to carry on. Little by little my mind grew accustomed to the idea and adjusted itself to this insensate rock; little by little I felt a vigorous strength pervading me; my fingers would lock in a crack, my toes find a hold on tiny projections. Several times I noticed that the rock had been hammered—traces of pitons used by earlier climbers. On this kind of pitch one either knocks in the necessary number of pitons—which I did not have—or, in spite of the tiny holds, one hoists oneself up in one go. That is, if one is in that certain uplifted mental and physical condition. So it is with the footballer who, for once, cannot put a foot wrong: he goes from one end of the field to the other, outwitting his opponents one by one, and scores an incomparable goal. This only happens on rare occasions; that day, I was lucky: I now felt in great form. I was not thinking of the Matterhorn, or its beauty, or its history, any more; I was completely absorbed in my climbing. I co-ordinated my strictly precise movements, which seemed almost to perform themselves. At times contentment consists in being deeply, completely happy without knowing why. I reached the halting-place, a sort of recess. For a long moment my eyes wandered over the grey rock. I was looking for a reliable crack in which to fix firmly the piton that I had kept to belay my companions with. One after the other, they rejoined me; after that arduous stretch we were glad to be together again.

By way of a groove on the left, in order to avoid the top of the projecting rock, we quickly reached a gloomy, dripping couloir-chimney. This traverse enabled us to survey the west; an ominous sky laden with black clouds was waiting on the horizon. Then a frantic race began!

We climbed as swiftly as possible—ledge, couloir, chimney . . . When I reached the summit ridge, the

storm was sullenly threatening. While I was belaying my two companions, my hair bristled, and first my ice-axe and then the rock began to vibrate. From time to time I was aware of almost palpable waves of electricity, propelled along by the wind.

It was late; seven-thirty in the evening, and it was August 10th. At that season the days have noticeably shortened, especially on stormy evenings. We wanted to get down and sleep at the Solvay hut so as to witness the sunrise over the Matterhorn and the peaks of the Valais the following day. However, the usual route leading there, though easy in good weather, becomes very tricky in a storm, when a climber, shaken by thunder and lightning, is in danger of falling off the slippery rock-slabs which become covered with snow. The Tête du Cervin is a perfect springboard at such times; it was there that Croz, Hadow, Hudson and Douglas fell . . . We know the dreadful story.

We moved quickly, though with the utmost caution. That sounds contradictory, but it is strictly true. What mysterious, secret force, apparently dormant in us, came to our aid? Side by side with the accumulation of difficulties and this danger that we so much disliked, we felt reserves of energy and skill, which every man carries within him and which reveal themselves only in great emergencies, coming to life deep within us. In spite of the crashing thunder, the blinding snow, the squalls of wind which jostled us, we experienced a solemn pleasure; the pleasure of maintaining our self-mastery and remaining calm and precise in spite of the perils. We had to move quickly, but at the same time avoid the slightest error for which we would have had to pay dearly.

It was eight in the evening, and very dark; in a few moments night enveloped us like an opening trap. We were suddenly plunged into a dense, bottomless darkness. Our descent became considerably slower.

After a short time, strange glimmerings appeared below us. My companions shouted to me: 'There's the hut! Look, they're signalling to us with lanterns!'

How I wished it were true! But I knew that 'Solvay' was at least 600 feet lower down, and that we could no longer reach it. My sole concern was to get as far as possible from the summit crest, where the firework display reserved for state occasions was in full swing; to lose altitude, and then to find a niche that would afford a little shelter. In the darkness, seeing nothing, feeling nothing but our blind feet and fingers placed on doubtful holds, we waited for the lightning flashes to enable us to take two or three steps. However, when the lightning streaked across the sky, its fierce light dazzled us violently; then from far off and far below darkness, total darkness would return.

From memory, we moved a foot, then a hand, on to holds glimpsed during the lightning-flash.

We halted under a sort of inclined slab that acted to some extent as a windbreak – a miserable bivouac. Still, we liked bivouacking. For some little time the weird glimmerings had increased in number around us; they were curious plumes of electricity. I had already seen some terrifying sights during storms – balls of fire as big as oranges rolling the length of the rock-face, bouncing off and bursting in a stunning thunder, or, at other times, the yellowish, then mauve zig-zag of the spark, accompanied by the smell of ozone; but never those delicate, fine, dancing plumes about eighteen inches high that came darting as if by magic on to the rocks. When the thunder crashed on the summit of the Matterhorn, they were suddenly extinguished. Then they returned, mysteriously and noiselessly, like fairies, and multiplied until the next discharge. What a fantastic, hectic ballet they danced around us!

Sometimes we were shaken by the thunder, but not very violently; it was on the summit crest of the Matterhorn that it crashed unceasingly. Right inside a laboratory of a kind he could never have imagined, Paul Beylier, an electrical engineer, delivered a lecture: 'The Matterhorn is an ideal lightning conductor. The earth's electrical charge flows by way of the arêtes up to the summit, where it joins with the electricity of the clouds.' It was so simple! And still the plumes returned to surround us, were extinguished at each thunderclap, gradually returned, were extinguished . . . After the lecture came songs. Strange how, at difficult moments, man loves to sing.

Beneath our rock we had some slight protection, but if we stuck a hand out from the windbreak, a plume appeared as a prolongation of each finger. Half-standing, half-sitting, doubled up as we were, our muscles stiffened

The Matterhorn and the clouds. Photo: Margaret Wunsch

very quickly; when we changed position, we were clothed in a luminous outer covering, like a cape with long, shining fur, while our heads were shaggy with sparks. 'Those golden filaments that surround you are very beautiful,' Paul Beylier informed us. We hastily got back to our perch under the windbreak.

Thus sheltered on a mountain overflowing with electricity, and having admitted that we were enjoying a remarkable spectacle, we finally spent a fantastic night.

Towards two in the morning the cloud base burst open beneath our feet. We saw, as if at the bottom of a well, the lights of Zermatt, and suddenly we were very cold. Down there, under roofs of larchwood and slate, the houses were nests of warmth. Up aloft, we were shivering, frozen to the bone. After a moment Zermatt sank out of sight, the clouds drowned its lights, and the fireworks began again.

However, to announce the end of the storm, snow began to fall. Jagged crystals whirled around us, stinging our faces and infiltrating everywhere. In the middle of the night the mountain turned white as in an hallucination. Above us, the cloud ceiling was pierced for a moment: a few stars appeared; but so distant, so uncertain, that our eyes quickly turned away from them. Up there, above the storm, shining for nothing, they were wasted. It began to snow again, and continued until first light. Towards five o'clock a grey light appeared on our right. A few glimmers of light arose, and the high peaks coloured timidly.

However, puffs of fresh wind were stretching the clouds. We shared a few pieces of nougat, a bit of sausage and some dried fruit, then we began the descent. It had a solemn quality. Was this due to the prestige of the Matterhorn, to that immaculate crest, or to the total silence after the tumult of the storm?

We were alone.

We moved with caution, for the snow that had fallen during the night hid the slippery verglas that covered the rocks. It was all within the rules of the game, and it was up to us to know it and take account of it. We were not tired, nor were we elated, but we were happy, as we had been the day before. We found pleasure in putting our

technical skill and our stamina to the test.

For a moment the light tints of the east turned pale, the wind slackened and the Valais range became sombre. Meanwhile, a cold wind sprang up again: through the mists, gaps of light warmed the mountain here and there, and gradually the weather improved.

It was noon when we reached the Hörnli hut. After the privations of the night, we sat down to lunch with pleasure. There was a joy within us for which there is no substitute. The thick walls of the hut, the bitter taste of the beer, the scalding soup, the fragrant smell of the ham, the local wine–how agreeable it all was, and how good it was to bite into fruit! Man's happiness is a simple thing. To bring about our great happiness that day, the mountain, during these past twenty-four hours, had thrown together all its resources– the beauty of the Matterhorn, its history, its easy and its acrobatic pitches; the fine weather, then the storm, then lunch in the Hörnli hut. But before all else there had been the friendship of the rope, without which the wonders of nature could be cold and dry.

MEDITATION

Another time I set out for the Matterhorn with Pierre Bichet and François Le Guen.

Having gone to Guido Rey's house again, while waiting for the weather to improve, and having roamed about the overcrowded mass of building that Cervinia is today, we went up to the Giomein and visited sheep-folds of extraordinary beauty, entirely built of dry stones and with vaulted ceilings. It was already autumn. The animals were no longer there. Then, as part of our walk, we went a little higher, looking at the Matterhorn, which could be seen from time to time through the clouds.

Just as Paul Beylier had been thrilled by the electrical phenomena during the storm, so François, a young geologist, talked to us about the formation of the mountains, and, more particularly, of the Matterhorn. True, I love climbing, but everything to do with the peaks interests me, whether it be modern climbs, technical problems, the history of the various conquests or vast meditations on the millennia that preceded us. The young geologist also gave us a lecture; he had the amphitheatre of Breuil for a lecture-hall, and two attentive pupils, Pierre and myself. We found it so

The summit of the Matterhorn: on the left, the Zmutt arête; facing, the west face; on the right, the Lion arête.
Photo: Bradford Washburn

interesting that at the end I asked him to write a note about it in simple terms as his 'lecture' had been . . .

'A mountain like the Matterhorn engenders in us, by reason of its imposing mass and the purity of its shape, a feeling of respect. It seems to us that this gigantic monument could personify the imperishable. However, things have not always been as they are now.

'In order to understand its formation better, this mountain must be considered together with the whole of which it forms a part – the chain of the Alps. 180 million years ago, in the place of this great mountain range there existed a deep sea in which thick layers of sediment were slowly deposited. The signs of these origins are to be found in the fossils picked up here and there, which are not, as Voltaire believed, sea-shells left by pilgrims, but the imprints of living organisms that populated these oceans of former times.

'About 90 million years ago, the bed of that ocean swelled up, initiating an upward movement which finally resulted in the emergence of a few islets, then in the creation of a chain, fragments of which gradually filled the declivities remaining at the edges. This process went on for 85 to 89 million years; in other words, it was very slow, and would have been imperceptible to an observer on the spot.

'From the time they appeared, the Alps were attacked by erosion, but the most significant phenomena, those that left their mark, were the four quaternary glaciations. A drop in the average temperature was enough to cause the glaciers to overflow on to the neighbouring regions, as the rate of thaw became less than that of the deposit of snow. On four occasions, during a period of a million years, the glaciers advanced, overflowing even the Jura and descending south of Lyons. These powerful movements planed the peaks and cut out the great valleys that we know today.

'It was these glaciations that cleared the Alps of milliards of cubic metres of matter under which they lay dormant. It was at that period that the Matterhorn must have come into being. However, during those millions of years of waiting, the mud deposited in the original sea had been transformed, matured. Reactions between molecules, migrations in the interior of matter, caused the appearance of minerals which collected in superimposed layers, transforming the original mud into structured rock. There was metamorphosis or recrystal-

lization of that mud, giving schists and gneiss. In the course of the folding of the strata, a harder stratum came to be placed on a softer where the Matterhorn stands; erosion was thus slowed up in the upper part and accelerated in the lower.

'In the original ice-cap, islets of rock appeared; then the glaciers, diminishing in volume by reason of the thaw, finally existed only on the sides of the mountains. On the Matterhorn this phenomenon was very regular and symmetrical, giving rise to four faces, each smoothed by a glacier, the harder, steeply-sloping stratum of the summit capping and protecting a softer, gently-sloping stratum. Nowadays, the glacial erosion has virtually ceased, but frost and thaw on shaly rock cause the mountain to be undermined everywhere, and let loose here and there the rock falls well known and feared by climbers, which tend constantly to level the terrain more and more.'

INTIMACY AND RESPECT

I have been up the Matterhorn many times, too, to make films and take photographs with my friends, the Tairraz'; there is no better way of getting to know a mountain thoroughly. One has to get up early and go to bed very late, for it is only when the light is tangential, that is, in the very early morning and at the end of the day, that features stand out in relief. One has to be patient, too, to wait for the correct lighting, and it is thanks to that that one discovers many different aspects of a single arête on a single face. We have been known to spend ten days at a stretch between the Hörnli hut and the summit when we were working for Walt Disney; sometimes we returned to the hut, sometimes we slept at the Solvay. We have observed the life of the Matterhorn, and seen the procession of the countless teams which follow one another in disciplined haste over the tricky stretches like an endless caterpillar and reform into groups elsewhere. One morning, in the space of ten minutes, there were fifteen people on the little platform of the Solvay hut at the foot of the Moseley slab. They were in two rows. Some of them were taking the opportunity to have a bit to eat, others to gain one or two places in the queue. The slab was being climbed by two climbers at once, moving up almost abreast. I remember that one of them slipped shortly after he started. Being quite unhurt by his fall, he set off again

On the Hörnli arête a number of rope-teams await their turn to climb the Moseley slab above the Solvay hut.
Photo: Gaston Rébuffat

immediately so as not to lose his place. On certain days the Matterhorn is so crowded! And yet on that day the weather was cloudy and unfavourable. But one has to look no further than the hut! We have known the Hörnli hut full to bursting, and have been turned away from the hotel because it was too late. So we went away, disgruntled, and found peace again by climbing the Matterhorn, alone by moonlight. It was a marvellous night. We were in good training, each of us having done the climb several times, and we were not roped, at any rate up to the Solvay. Each of us went at his own pace, borne along by the silence and our reveries.

Now it is the end of September. The weather is magnificent. Paul has telephoned me: he has four days' holiday, let us go to Zermatt; at this season there should not be too many people on the Matterhorn; we will do the classic crossing, up by the Hörnli arête and down by the Lion arête.

We will follow the course of the sun.

It is a pleasure to see again this village of the Valais, which, despite the invasion, has contrived to preserve its character. As we alight from the train in front of the Station Hotel, we see Bernard Biner, laughing-eyed, always full of charm, always ready to be of service; higher up we meet a group of guides, among them Eddy Petrig, with whom I have often been roped, then Bernard Seiler, deep of voice and tall of stature, who carries on the tradition. There is a cordial greeting from each. Then we start out for the hut. Many things have changed since the 'golden age', since Whymper's comings and goings, but the higher one climbs—in spite of oneself, in spite of everything—the more one is steeped in the atmosphere and is conscious of the full weight of the Matterhorn's presence and its past.

The hut is a wonderful place for meetings, sometimes planned, sometimes unexpected. The caravans climb, descend, cross on to the Italian side . . . . The Matterhorn is not only a pyramid, it is an *ambiance*.

The following morning, or rather, when it was still completely dark, we were already up. In mountaineering,

of course, there is the joy of climbing, but before that there is the joy of sharing in the great spectacles, the great experiences of nature. Colours appear in the east, heralding the sun, which will soon touch the peak.

Now, we are moving up the arête. On the right are the Weisshorn, the Zinalrothorn, the Ober Gabelhorn, the Dent Blanche; behind us the Mischabels and the Monte Rosa, the Lyskamm, Castor and Pollux, the Breithorn; on the left, the Théodule and Italy. The weather is superb. We are happy to be climbing, relaxed, over these easy rocks. However, the pleasure is not limited to the climb alone, it is more of a pilgrimage than an ascent. The Matterhorn? This is a name that resounds in our hearts, for it is the historic mountain *par excellence*. Over these rocks the founders of our family blazed the trail, and we think of them as one thinks of grandfathers who were at once hard and generous.

We reach the Solvay hut, perched there on the narrow arête, a tiny shelter that has saved so many lives. We carry on, with sometimes Paul, sometimes myself in the lead. I love to lead, but I also like to give that proof of confidence and that pleasure to my companions whenever they can do it in safety. Although it is the end of the season, there are still about a dozen teams making the ascent, ropes with guides and without guides, ropes of Swiss, Germans, Japanese, Americans . . . . Most of them are on their way up, but some are already coming down. In my innermost heart I think: 'People climb the Matterhorn for all sorts of reasons; but first of all because it is *the Matterhorn.*' It should not be approached in the hope of having an interesting climb; the rock is often in bad condition; after climbing the snow slope that leads to the Shoulder, and when one reaches the Tête du Cervin, it becomes better, but then it is festooned with fixed ropes. No, when climbing the Matterhorn, one must, in one's heart of hearts, allow oneself to be guided by the charm of that enchanted peak; and if, for a brief moment, one thinks of the climb as such, one may also recall that Michel Croz, Whymper and their companions passed that way—without fixed ropes.

Higher up, less steep slopes lead to the Swiss summit. It is fine today, unlike the evening we came off the Furggen, and we have ample time, for we want to spend the night on the mountain.

At the end of the day, by way of the aery crest that dominates the south face on one side and the north face on

the other, and which passes the little notch where the cross is situated, we go to the Italian summit. We are following the course of the sun. The air is pure. What peace is here!

Now we prepare the bivouac. Thirty feet below the Italian summit there is a little platform, suspended like a balcony in the empty sky. Here we will spend the night. We want to bivouac so that we may learn more about our mountain, and later on in the night to hear its life pulsating. It is not enough just to pass on our way; we will climb to the summit and descend from it at moderate speed, but we will also dwell awhile on the enchanted peak.

We are alone. In the daytime, at the height of the season it is not rare on some days for more than a hundred people to make the ascent; I have seen it. In the autumn, and even more in the evening, the great mountain regains its true dimensions, its marvellous solitude, its incorruptible silence, and mystery dwells there once again.

In the valleys it is already very dark. Here, at 14,400 feet, we receive the last caresses of the sun.

Paul, so happy to be there, is in high spirits. Over there on the horizon, in a halo of clouds, the sun, unflaggingly pursues its course. For a long time we remain silent; each man to his meditation.

In the first light of morning, like islands of another world, the mountains emerge from the clouds, while to the east, behind our backs, a great feast is in preparation: the return of the life-giving sun.

Without haste we set off again by way of the Italian arête . . . .

*

So, by day and by night, in fine weather and in storm, fast or slowly, preoccupied by the business of climbing or plunged in history, savouring the landscape and savouring friendship, we have climbed, lived among and descended these arid and apparently indifferent rocks.

left-hand page
In the séracs of the glacier. Photo: Pierre Tairraz

pages 216-217
On the Hörnli arête during the filming of *Third Man on the Mountain* by Walt Disney. Photo: Françoise Rébuffat

pages 218-219
The Matterhorn cross and the Italian summit.
Photo: Pierre Tairraz

pages 220-221
The summit of the Matterhorn seen from the west through the sea of clouds. Photo: Bradford Washburn

Therein lies our tribute of love. It is swallowed up in the extraordinary sum of time, energy, courage, struggle and generosity that all men have brought to the Matterhorn. And it matters little whether they have climbed the north face or the normal route, the Furggen arête, directly by way of the overhangs or by going round them: the methods and the ways are different, but the motivating force is the same. On one occasion the Matterhorn was climbed by a blind man. How well one can understand!

The Earth, in its extraordinary gestation, presented men with the gift of a wonderful mountain. Those men in return have loved it more than any other!

Imprimé par l'I.I.A.G.
Bergame - Italie
Dépôt légal n° 6601
2ᵉ trimestre 1973 - 23-71-2328-01